# PRAISE FOR
# FAITH STORYTELLERS

"I'm so excited for the impact this book will have in encouraging people to tell their faith stories."

— *Diane Haskins, author of faith story "You are my beloved"*

"I never thought it possible to whittle and shape my story into an 8-minute time frame, but it has made all the difference. My confidence is stronger, my story more portable. Now I do not fear that I will lose my listener or burden him or her with too much too quickly. I'm able to engage and leave an impression that (I hope) is lasting and leaves the individual asking: Who is this great God who heals such deep burdens? God's story is written into each of our lives and I'm more grateful than ever to share a small piece of His greater craftsmanship."

— *Abbie Kampman, author of faith story "Finding redemption after a tragic loss"*

"I was nervous and unsure of what I had to offer through my story. When compared to others, I considered my story to be insignificant. My faith journey has been a slow 25-year development — nothing out of the ordinary. However, this class refined my ability to see how God has worked within me. The class exposed intimate moments between God and I that I pushed aside as coincidental. Looking back, I learned that anything involving God is powerful, meaningful and worth sharing for His glory."

— *Elyse Webb, author of faith story "If God is bigger than death, then God is bigger than cancer"*

*Faith Storytellers: Unleash the Power of Your Story*

# Faith Storytellers

## UNLEASH THE POWER OF YOUR STORY

*Written and edited by*

## MACKENZIE RYAN WALTERS

*Christian imprint of StoryStruck Marketing*

Published in West Des Moines, Iowa, by Faith Storytellers, the Christian imprint of StoryStruck Marketing. Contact the publisher through storystruckmarketing.com.

Scripture quotations taken from the Holy Bible, New International Version (R), NIV (R), Copyright (C) 1973, 1978, 1984, 2011 by Biblica Inc. Due to the nature of this book, other translations of the Holy Bible may have been used.

The stories included in this book were included with written permission from the authors and edited according to Faith Storytellers style and guidelines. The authors have attested that these are true, first-person stories about their faith.

ISBN - Paperback
979-8-9900304-0-4
ISBN - Hardcover
979-8-9900304-2-8
ISBN - Ebook
979-8-9900304-1-1

# BONUS: STORYTELLING RESOURCES

A reporter's notebook is full of tidbits that never make it to print, which is why I curated some of my favorite resources, research, and references to accompany this book.

"Faith Storytellers: Unleash the Power of Your Story" is everything I know about the art and craft of faith storytelling. But as I researched, tested, and wrote this book, I discovered far more than I could ever include within these pages.

That's why I'm opening my proverbial "reporter's notebook" to you on the Faith Storytellers website: **faithstoryteller.org/resources**. This digital library will help you:

### Facilitate discussion:
- Book club discussion guide
- Storytelling personality quiz
- Additional storytelling resources

### Share your story:
- Gratitude story worksheet with prompts
- Tips for public speaking
- Writing resources, tips, and advice

### Dive deeper:
- Bible verses printouts
- Miracles and other faith stories
- Resources such as books, podcasts, and more

Find these resources and more at **faithstoryteller.org/resources**.

# DEDICATION

*To Andy Walters,*
*thank you for encouraging and*
*supporting me on this journey.*

# CONTENTS

# PREFACE

I was fortunate to work as a newspaper reporter for 14 years at a time when newsrooms around the country were declining in size. As a college student, I visited the storied Washington Post newsroom, and a grizzled copy editor warned our class it was a shrinking industry and not to do it. But I didn't care.

Journalism offered me a front-row seat to history. I enjoyed meeting new people, learning about their lives, and sharing stories with the community.

Asking questions came naturally to me, and I thrived as a community and then education reporter. I wanted to understand what was happening and what caused it. I earned recognition for investigative journalism as I dug into public records and asked officials hard questions. I spotted trends, broke news, and won a national reporting award while living and working in Florida — a state so known for its news cycle that it's often seen as a training ground for national reporters.

Writing? That wasn't as easy. An editor once told me journalists are either natural reporters or natural writers, and rarely both. But the good news? Both can be learned. That was certainly true for me.

Thanks to the talented editors I worked with over the years, my dedication to the craft, and more than a decade of writing day in and day out, I can now string a story together on cue. In fact, structuring a story — choosing what to include and what to leave out — became my favorite part of the writing process.

I was eager to use and share my knowledge when I arrived at the Des Moines Register, considered one of the best newspapers in the country.

When the newspaper launched a live storytelling series, I volunteered to coach everyday people on how to tell a first-person story.

Storytellers were understandably nervous about sharing a personal and vulnerable story with a few hundred — and eventually, more than a thousand — people in the audience. More people saw them on television, thanks to a partnership with a local station, and in the print and online paper.

Setting the storytellers up for success was crucial. I practiced a version of "tough love," requiring storytellers to tell me the story from memory; you'll see why in the following chapters. It may seem kind to allow someone a "script" to read or refer to onstage, but I believe it ultimately acts as a crutch. While it relieves much of the anxiety around public speaking, it also prevents the storytellers from reaching their full potential and the audience from fully absorbing their story.

As a listener, it's hard to follow a story read from a piece of paper. The tone, speed, and inflection are different when you speak it out loud. It's also hard to have the discipline, as a speaker, to memorize your story if you know you have your notes. So far, I've been right. At the newspaper's events and the faith storytelling nights we held at my church, each storyteller remembered what to say onstage. Each told their story by heart.

With each storytelling event, I started to see what made some stories work and others fall apart. While the story arc itself was significant, especially the all-important ending, success was determined by how the story was structured and delivered. Over time, I identified key elements of a short story and saw the results of my coaching in real time.

Sitting in the audience, I immediately sensed what worked and what fell flat. Did the audience understand the chronology of events? Did they get the jokes? Did they lean in, wanting to hear how the story resolved, or did they lean back, wishing it was over already?

I explained why storytellers needed to change their structure, details, or delivery in my storytelling coaching sessions. I found myself repeating the same advice. My knowledge became the foundation of the Faith Storytellers Framework I share in this book.

One step led to the next. I taught a faith storytelling class at my church and wrote a workbook that structured my thoughts and standardized my guidance. I then tested the concepts while editing personal faith stories for faithstorytellers.org.

The storytellers I worked with were beginning their journey as Christian writers and speakers. Despite being new to the relationship of writer and editor, they rose to the occasion and took my (hopefully gentle) recommendations and revisions in stride.

Years later, when I asked permission to include their stories in Part II of this book, many shared how writing and revising their faith story was a small yet significant step to their development as writers and speakers, authors and Bible teachers.

While they never took the faith storytelling class I taught at my church, the framework I shared with them — and now with you — translated seamlessly. They built skills and confidence. More importantly, they shifted their perspective. They embraced the identity of being a faith storyteller.

I put my passion for faith storytelling aside for a few years to navigate life after journalism. After 14 years as a newspaper reporter working for increasingly prestigious and demanding papers, it was time to make a change.

I had taken a few University of Iowa MBA courses to explore my interest in business, which seemed more exciting from the inside than writing about it from a journalist's perspective. I'd double-majored in journalism and economics at American University in Washington, D.C., I reminded myself. It was time to lean into my curiosity.

For one evening class, my professor explained how every industry has a life cycle. Industries could be in the startup phase, the growth or maturity phases, or decline, the last phase before they no longer exist.

Newspapers, the textbook claimed as I followed along with the lecture, were the prime example of a declining industry. That was something I knew intellectually yet didn't digest emotionally until that moment. Never mind the dozen or more rounds of layoffs I "survived" or the cost-cutting restructures that forced me to reapply for my job. Twice.

There it was, in black and white, the reality I was avoiding. I shifted uncomfortably in my seat, suddenly aware of my precarious situation.

Somewhere between the drive home and the next staff meeting about further cuts, I made my decision. The career I dedicated the better part of my 20s and 30s to was over. It was time to figure out what was next. As Ernest Hemingway once said, "Newspaper work will not harm a young writer and could help him if he gets out of it in time."

I launched my own business, StoryStruck Marketing, in 2019 with the goal of bringing a journalistic approach to business marketing. The idea of telling your story was already catching on with the business community, but few were doing it well. As any entrepreneur would tell you, seeing the need and launching the business was the exciting part. Building it took more energy and focus than I expected!

A few years passed before I felt a quiet nudge during a prayer session at my church. A direction to turn the Faith Storytellers class and blog into a book. I could feel my chest tighten. Wasn't I busy enough as a business owner, wife, and bonus mom? Hadn't I already gone down a book-writing path once before, only to be disappointed and a bit disillusioned with the publishing world?

Fear filled my heart. I imagined rejection and criticism. I wrestled with God in my quiet time, listing all the ways why I felt writing and publishing a book was a terrible idea.

A decade before, I had talked to other journalists-turned-authors, applied for and was a finalist for a journalism fellowship, and pitched a book agent who was initially interested in my premise. But everywhere I turned, I found dead ends. Everyone told me not to write a book, that the industry wasn't what it used to be, that it would be a lot of work without much reward. I finally quit. If I were to write a book, I decided, the book would need to find me.

And find me it did — two, in fact! While finalizing edits for "Faith Storytellers: Unleash the Power of Your Story," a business leader reached out to ask if I would ghostwrite a book for his team.

He had worked with a book coach, but since he wasn't a professional writer, he'd struggled to implement her advice. That didn't surprise me at all, I told him. He was a numbers guy and spent decades refining his craft; building up a similar level of mastery in writing and editing (as editing, as every writer knows, is the key to good writing) would take a similar amount of time and dedication.

Surprisingly, I fell in love with ghostwriting, which includes in-depth interviews and research, creating a structure for his stories and wisdom, and writing it for his target audience. I saw his vision and how giving away his knowledge would benefit others. Plus, it could catapult his business by positioning him and his co-authors as experts in the eyes of the public and differentiate him from his competition.

Helping authors write and launch their books was an avenue I never saw coming, nor one I would have pursued without God's frustrating nudge to shift directions.

I'm glad I did. My business, StoryStruck Marketing, is dedicated to workshopping, ghostwriting, and publishing nonfiction books that make a difference. Personal or professional, Christian or secular, business or memoir. No other medium forces you to clarify your thoughts so specifically — or concentrate so intently on your readers — as a book.

What began as a desire to capture the goodness of God and the love of his people transformed and grew in a way I never expected. Looking back, the decision to leave journalism now seemed inevitable. Yet I wouldn't have believed it at the time: how the same technology that prompted the newspaper industry's decline would propel me into a new career.

In this book, I share everything I know about faith storytelling. In Part I, I walk you through key storytelling principles, a step-by-step framework, and common missteps to avoid. I illustrate these with stories from my own life. Since I moved frequently as a journalist, I've included a timeline on the next page for quick reference.

In the appendix, you'll find helpful resources, including a quiz to assess your natural storytelling tendencies and quick references to the Faith Storytellers Framework and Faith Story Guardrails. These are also available online at **faithstoryteller.org/resources**.

In addition, you can learn more about any of the 40 authors in the Bios of Faith Storytellers section in the appendix. Many have their own blogs, websites, or books, which you'll find listed there. Please connect with them directly if their story resonates with you.

I hope this book encourages you to explore, write, and share your faith story. Please know your story can and will make a difference — although I doubt we'll see the full impact this side of heaven. And I pray that as you read the following true, first-person stories of faith, you better understand God the Father, God the Son, and God the Holy Spirit.

# TIMELINE

**1982–2000,** Grew up in the western suburbs of Minneapolis

**2000–2004,** American University to study journalism and economics in Washington, D.C.

**2004–2005,** The Gazette in Frederick, Maryland

**2005–2008,** St. Cloud Times in St. Cloud, Minnesota

**2008–2010,** Statesman Journal in Salem, Oregon

**2010–2015,** Florida Today in Melbourne, Florida

**2015–2019,** The Des Moines Register in Iowa

**2019–Present,** StoryStruck Marketing in Iowa

# PART I:
# HOW TO TELL YOUR FAITH STORY

*"Ask and it will be given to you; seek and you will find; knock and the door will be opened to you. For everyone who asks receives; the one who seeks finds; and to the one who knocks, the door will be opened." (New International Version)*

*"Continue to ask, and God will give to you. Continue to search, and you will find. Continue to knock, and the door will open for you." (International Children's Bible)*

— *Matthew 7:7-8*

CHAPTER 1

# THE STORY GOD IS WRITING IN THE WORLD

On a sunny Florida day in 2011, a young grandfather entered the newspaper's window-paned lobby. The man's shirt showed his occupation as a bug exterminator, but his face revealed more: the seriousness of his task.

I sat beside him, glancing out the window before we began. I could see a retainer pond and an alligator sunning itself. Behind it were trees that hid the Indian River and barrier islands. A picturesque setting that didn't match our conversation's tone.

Richard explained his grandson was severely burned in a house fire in North Carolina a few years before. Isaac was 2 and sustained second- and third-degree burns on 80% of his body. When his father pulled him out of the house, he wasn't breathing. After months of intense medical treatment, his family is thankful for him to be alive.

Isaac started kindergarten in North Carolina, but his classmates feared his scars. Remnants of the fire covered his face and head, where his hair should have been, and across his arms and legs.

Isaac couldn't focus. He grew fearful of school. His classmates called him names, shoved him, pushed him. When a fire alarm went off, he ran away.

The family moved to Florida for a fresh start. Isaac's family talked to his new teacher, and they enlisted the help of the local fire department to accompany him as an "honorary fireman" on his first day.

The grandfather wanted to do more. He believed the community should know this little boy was loved and worthy of acceptance. Parents could talk to their children about how to treat Isaac if they saw him at the park or grocery store.

"Will you write about Isaac's first day?" he asked. I nodded. Of course I would.

The most meaningful stories of my journalism career came at moments without breathing room in my schedule. But my calendar sorted itself out when I talked to my editors about Isaac. It always did. Later, I recognized this as divine timing, a rearranging of events and meetings where God found a way to put his priorities first.

A few days later, Richard shared Isaac's story with me, acting as a family liaison to describe what Isaac's father, Brad, struggled to articulate.

The fire ravaged the home of Isaac's great-grandmother, where his family was staying at the time. A news report said Isaac's father was doing home maintenance, using acetone and gas to remove glue that held down carpet he was attempting to remove.

Brad pulled Isaac out first. He wasn't breathing, and his mother did CPR. Brad ran back to pull out his daughter, Isaac's sister, and a third time to rescue his mother-in-law.

Brad was about to go in a fourth time when firefighters stopped him. It was too dangerous to go inside.

As I read the report, I couldn't imagine the pain of that moment, watching flames engulf his home — his wife's grandmother and sister inside. Their deaths imminent as the flames grew.

Richard told me it was an accident. But that didn't take away the hunch of Brad's shoulders, or his sparse words when asked about Isaac's challenges. Officials had determined it wasn't his fault, but I still sensed his feelings of guilt when I looked into his eyes.

## WELCOMING A NEW CLASSMATE

Everyone was in position on Isaac's first day of school. I stood in the cafeteria behind tables of kindergartners, their teachers hovering nearby. The students buzzed with excitement, eager to welcome their new classmate, nervous about what to expect when he arrived.

Across the cafeteria, Isaac walked through the door. Students started to clap. I could see Isaac's apprehension. He leaned into a nearby firefighter, saw the rows of eyes, and ducked behind the cafeteria's door to hide.

A teacher diverted the students' attention by asking if they remembered their first day of school. If they could relate to Isaac's feelings. The kindergartners nodded. It was still a recent memory.

As Isaac walked toward the group, with firefighters and family on either side, students began to whisper.

*Are the scars contagious?*

Colds and the flu spreads between people.

*Will the scars catch fire?*

They'd been told not to play with matches in case something caught fire.

*If I touch him, will the scars jump onto me?*

The children were filling in gaps in their knowledge, and bugs were a constant challenge in this Florida climate.

If the adults in the room didn't create space to ask questions, didn't address those questions directly, and didn't speak confidently about what was and was not true, their questions would linger. Eventually, these young minds would draw their own, likely incorrect, conclusions.

## UNDERSTANDING THEIR CLASSMATE

The firefighters left the cafeteria first, telling students to treat Isaac with the same respect they would treat a firefighter.

His family was next. His father gave him one last hug and told Isaac he loved him. Isaac's teacher took him by the hand and they walked to her classroom. The rest of her students followed behind.

His teacher, Kathy, showed Isaac his new desk. Overwhelmed, he ducked underneath.

An experienced instructor with a calm and peaceful demeanor, Kathy was born for this day. She let Isaac be and directed the rest of her students to the carpet for a story. Then she pulled out a newspaper clipping about a kitten named Khloe.

A few weeks before, my colleague Rick wrote a story about Khloe, a 10-week-old kitten who survived a house fire in the nearby city of

Palm Bay. Her eyes were badly burned, her skin and fur singed from smoke. Kathy pointed to the picture of Khloe and a shelter volunteer taking care of her.

Students that age relate to animals, and the timing couldn't have been better for making a simple point. I watched as Kathy helped her students understand Isaac's story through Khloe's.

"The lady still likes her," said James, one of the students, of the volunteer holding Khloe in the picture. "She's smiling. She wasn't afraid of her." Other students nodded in agreement.

Kathy smiled. She pulled out a picture book and continued the day.

A few minute later, Isaac crawled out from under his desk and moved toward his classmates. Then he stopped, unsure.

"Isaac! Isaac!" one of them said, waving Isaac over. "Come sit by me."

## WHEN GOD WORKS SILENTLY

As a journalist, I talked with sources, scoured public records, and tuned my ear to the community's rumblings. I also witnessed historic events: the last space shuttle launches, court case decisions with national attention, and the beginnings of presidential campaigns. But the most significant stories — stories that moved me, taught me, showed me the goodness of people and the goodness of God — found me.

When I reflect on the thousands of stories I wrote during my 14 years as a journalist, I cherish Isaac's. To me, it's a story of how far love will go. How Isaac's family loved him so much, they moved to a new state to give him a second chance. How firefighters and teachers came together to care for him. How his classmates, led by the adults in their lives, put their fears aside and embraced their new friend on his first day.

Is it a story of faith? God wasn't mentioned in my newspaper article. I don't recall hearing his name in the public school or during the conversations I had. Yet I believe God was there, his presence known by the love and kindness shared.

I didn't have the words to articulate it then, as I was still learning about my relationship with God. But I do now. What I saw was an outpouring of love and compassion for a scared child, epitomizing 1 John 4:7-8: "Dear friends, let us love one another, for love comes from God ... because God is love."

## DESPITE THE SUFFERING

There are so many questions I can't answer about Isaac's story. I don't know why the house fire happened, although investigators determined what caused the spark and fueled the flames. Why two people died in the accident. Why Isaac and his family suffered.

Sharing stories such as Isaac's is why I became a journalist. While my colleagues were fascinated by true crime or political power, I wanted to see the goodness in people. I wanted to understand how ordinary people walked through extraordinary circumstances and kept their hope alive.

I was looking for stories of God's work in the world — evidence of his goodness and provision and divine timing. The more I looked for him, the more I saw God's involvement in everyday moments. As my faith grew, I wanted to read stories of God's goodness, whether he was mentioned or not. They were challenging to find.

In modern storytelling, whether in books, movies, or news stories, darkness fights for our attention. "If it bleeds, it leads," as the saying goes. It's why TV news airs crime stories at the top of each broadcast. It's why I wrote more stories about wrongdoing and fewer articles about good works when editors began ranking online page views.

After moving to Iowa, I found an outlet for sharing stories after co-founding a live event series where we coached everyday people to go onstage and tell a true, first-person story in front of a live audience. While many of the storytellers shared stories that contained darkness, they did not dwell on it. Instead, they focused on the meaning of the experience and how it affected their view of the world. It was an empowering, refreshing way to share stories. I was hooked.

I wanted the storytelling events to succeed, and they did: Our team helped the series grow from an audience of a hundred people to selling out a theater with more than a thousand seats. But the more it grew, the more I wanted storytellers to talk about their faith. It was something I could occasionally include, such as when I hosted an event called "Everyday Miracles," but not an approach a secular production could sustain.

When I shared this with my pastor, he invited me to develop and teach a faith storytelling class at our church. During the multiweek classes in our church basement, I encouraged faith storytellers to seek out the story God is writing in their lives. The story God is sharing with the world through them.

My experience proves every Christian has a story to tell, and everyone can tell it if they follow a few faith storytelling principles. I developed the **Faith Storytellers Framework, which teaches five steps anyone can take** to craft a short, first-person story about their faith and share it in a public setting. I'll go into more depth later about how to walk through each step, including how to work with your natural storytelling tendencies.

If you are a leader who wants to bring more stories of God into your community, this book is for you. If you are a writer, a speaker, a pastor, a small group leader, a ministry volunteer, or a passionate community member, it's for you, too. Maybe you teach a class, are asked to share your testimony, or want to have your story ready when asked about your faith.

It doesn't matter your position or status. What matters is your heart for the truth, following an intentional process, and understanding and applying the structure I explain in the following chapters. Before you write your faith story, I encourage you to read a few (if not all!) of the 40 stories in Part II of this book. Each serves as an example of the framework. But more than that, each story is a glimpse into God's intimate and personal love for the storyteller — and for you.

## FAITH STORYTELLERS FRAMEWORK

**Step 1: Pray for guidance** on what true, first-person story to share about your faith.

Consider praying, "God, what story have you given me to share with others as a gift, with no expectation of return?"

**Step 2: Divide your story into three scenes: A beginning, a middle where something changes, and an ending** that shares your beliefs about God. Often, your beginning will be the opposite of your resolution.

The last part of your story is your Story Anchor or central point. Limit yourself to one. Your ending should stay in the first person through the last word. If you're unsure, try finishing with the phrase: "What I know to be true about God is …"

**Step 3: Create a narrative sequence in each scene** using this format: description (time and place), action, and reaction.

Add details using one of your five senses (touch, hearing, smell, taste, sight).

**Step 4: Add divine details that show how God revealed himself to you.** Refine your story and check it against the Faith Story Guardrails, which are explained in the next section. Review your spelling, grammar, and word usage.

**Step 5: Prepare your story to share.** Practice saying it out loud from memory if you plan to speak it. Read it out loud to yourself if you are sharing it through writing.

Ask a trusted friend what parts to refine or clarify to help someone who doesn't know you understand what you're trying to convey. I've compiled questions I often asked as a journalist to complete this task, which I share at **faithstoryteller.org/resources**.

## CREATING STORY BOUNDARIES

Stories are powerful. Just as Khloe the kitten's story brought understanding to Isaac's classmates, your story can deepen relationships and foster healing. But I've also seen stories do the opposite: used to condemn or criticize, weaponized with guilt or shame, or as propaganda or a means to control.

That's why I also created guardrails to protect the emotional and spiritual safety of the faith storyteller, the people in their story, and those who receive it.

While the Faith Storytellers Framework will help you construct your story — similar to how scaffolding will help you build a building — the Faith Story Guardrails keep you and the people around you safe.

I never thought about guardrails, except occasionally while hiking and coming to a platform on the edge of a cliff with majestic views.

Their importance became clear while I was making the final edits for this book. It was the fall of 2023, and I was working from home. Deep in thought, I was startled by my phone's ring.

"Hey," I said to my husband. But he didn't respond. Instead, I heard a woman's voice. She introduced herself as a chaplain for one of the hospitals in downtown Des Moines.

Andy was in the emergency room, she explained. He seemed fine, although the doctors were still treating him. There had been a work accident. He had fallen 9 feet. Could I come?

While gathering my things, I glanced at my phone and saw multiple missed texts from his co-workers. I blinked back tears and tried to wipe the image of him in a wheelchair from my mind.

The chaplain met me in the lobby and ushered me into the room. Doctors hovered nearby. Andy was on his back, a brace around his neck.

Again, I blinked away tears as I pieced together what happened, thanking God he wasn't paralyzed or worse. The trauma doctors were clear: A fall could be life-threatening, even if the person seemed fine at the time, but the CT scan showed Andy was in the clear.

It had started like any other home remodeling project; they were working on a garage and were using scaffolding to reach above the door. Tired from long days at work and two back-to-back weekends of National Guard duty, my husband stood firmly on the platform when he mindlessly stepped back.

His leg didn't bump into a railing, however. No guardrails were boxing him in. Instead, his foot planted him on a platform that wasn't there. He fell, hitting his head and landing on his back.

Yet God protected him: Andy landed on grass, not the driveway, and he broke two "wings" of his spine bones, a minor injury compared with what could have happened. The doctors assured us the bones should heal on their own.

When his boss called me to express his sympathy, he assured me safety was the most important part of their job. They would spare no expense, he said. They wouldn't let clients push for faster completion or less expensive bills to cut safety corners.

Overwhelmed and emotionally exhausted, I thanked him for calling. As I hung up, I hoped what he said was true. Not a philosophical truth that was trotted out when something such as this happened, but a truth that was lived out with conviction and everyday application. That he would hold firm to his promise to take safety precautions not just next time but every time. Even if they seemed unnecessary in the moment.

While structural guardrails protect you from physical risks, **Faith Story Guardrails safeguard you from relational risks.** As a journalist, I knew how to spot and avoid certain pitfalls. Others I blundered through before learning from my mistakes. After talking with church leaders, I added or adjusted these guardrails to align with our beliefs and faith communities.

## FAITH STORY GUARDRAILS

- **I feel peace about how my story has unfolded so far.** I can share my story with composure and compassion.

- **I am willing to share my story with courage and vulnerability.** I am an imperfect person in a relationship with imperfect people. I have a perfect God.

- **I can share my story in a "PG" or "PG-13" way.** It may include the darkness, but it doesn't dwell on it. Instead, it focuses on how God worked in the situation or the light he brought.

- **My story is safe for me and the people in my story.** It does not allege wrongdoing by another or criticize or condemn others. It aligns with my church values and beliefs.

- **If needed, I am comfortable using a metaphor** instead of dwelling on the dark details or how I was wronged. Instead, I may focus on how I felt and name the emotions I was experiencing at the time.

- **I am the keeper of my story.** Because of this, my story is in the first person throughout. It uses "me," "my," "mine," and "I."

- **My story avoids teaching** or telling others what to do or what to believe ("you" or "your"). I've framed these, instead, as my approach to living or my personal belief or conviction.

- **My story avoids preaching,** which explains common beliefs or spiritual truths that universally apply ("our" or "we"). I've framed these, instead, as my personal belief about how God works in the world.

- **My story focuses on my relationship with God, not other people.** My Story Anchor, or main point, is grounded in my relationship with God and how he revealed himself to me.

- **I have only one main point in my story,** which is in my resolution. I acknowledge I have many stories to share, but I am focusing on only one.

- **My story brings resolution to the beginning.** My story's ending may be the opposite of my story's beginning. It concludes in the first person and answers the question: What do I know to be true about God that I didn't before?

- **I have agency over how long or short it is.** I have decided to share a short story that is 700 to 1,200 words when written or six to eight minutes when spoken.

- **I am ready to give my story away as a gift.** My story's value is not based on the number of people who read or hear it, nor is its value based on how people react after I share it. God already values my story.

## SHARING YOUR FAITH THROUGH STORIES

The most powerful way to share your faith is through your personal story. That means starting with and sticking to a first-person narrative (I, me, my, and mine). Free of the pressure to live or act a certain way, which is created when you speak in second person (you or your), audience members can be curious about a first-person story without having to agree.

When a storyteller uses language that assumes common beliefs (our, we), or tells someone what to do or believe (you, your), the opposite happens. The storyteller loses their attention. I have seen audience members lean back in their chairs as if to create emotional distance. They look at their watch or phone to distract themselves from what I assume they perceive as a lecture.

In the polarizing world of today, with a thousand media options at our fingertips, it's easy to go a whole day or year only consuming information that aligns with our convictions. A simple challenge to our beliefs can feel like an assault. For the storyteller, the difference is subtle. For the audience, it's the gulf between two mountains, a cliff of belief and of unbelief. When you tell someone what to do or believe, the listener feels shoved toward the cliff — and they resist.

A first-person story is the bridge. By sharing your story of belief, you implicitly invite the listener to take the first step. You share doubts you had about the strength of the bridge, your experience crossing it with the help of God, and how living on the mountain of belief changed your life. Then you ask the Holy Spirit to give the audience courage to take their next step.

**That's why the Faith Storytellers Framework does not include a "moral to the story," which morphs the story into a lesson or sermon.** Pastors share stories as part of their sermons, so it's easy to become confused about the difference. Think of it this way: Sermons teach you how or why God works, while stories tell you who God is, based on the evidence of your personal experience.

Your faith story is about your relationship with God. The Faith Storytellers Framework will ask you to act as a journalist and to look for evidence of God at work in your life. I pray that, as you examine the details of your story, God will reveal insight about how he has expressed and will continue to express his love to you.

A metaphor I often use is how **God is like the wind. I can't see the wind, but I can see its influence.** The leaves shift and the tree branches move. Sometimes the wind howls against my home, determined to be heard.

But most of the time, the wind is a breeze so soft I can easily forget it's there unless I stop and look for it. My desire to see God at work is the same: a journey of asking questions, then listening and watching for how God reveals himself in the significant events of my life and the little details I might otherwise miss.

## KEY CONCEPTS AND APPLICATION

- **God is writing a story in our lives.** If we pause and ask God where he was in our story, he will show us. Whether our story unfolds in a church pew or arenas seemingly void of his presence, we can trust God is with us.

- **Every Christian has a story of faith to share,** regardless of how dramatic it is by secular standards. God may have moved silently through the goodness of his people, or he may have joined with you in grief or suffering, or he may have made his presence known in a straightforward or life-changing way.

- **The Faith Storytellers Framework** provides a structure you can follow to craft your faith story to share. By starting with the first step — praying for guidance on what story to tell — and following each step in order, you can construct a meaningful, first-person story about your faith.

- **Guardrails keep us safe** in real life. Not having them increases our risk of hurting ourselves or others by accident. Following a few guardrails in the faith storytelling process can keep yourself, the people in your story, and your audience emotionally and spiritually safe.

- **God is with us daily,** but he may move quietly or gently or anonymously. Part of the faith storytelling process is looking for how God has worked in your life in seemingly ordinary — and occasionally, in extraordinary — ways.

CHAPTER 2

# MUSTARD SEEDS AND MIRACLES

When I arrived at college on the East Coast in 2000, I wore the coolest jeans my waitressing money could afford. They were boot cut, light denim, and I felt like a rock star when I wore them. They were everywhere in my home state of Minnesota. But when I arrived in Washington, D.C., for classes, everyone was sporting dark jeans.

I stood out, which an English professor only emphasized when he called my home a "flyover state" on the first day of class. A few weeks later, after discovering I was from Minnesota, a political science professor asked if I wore Keds.

I was desperate to fit in, to feel like I belonged. I looked forward to Friday and Saturday nights when upperclassmen invited students to parties off campus. I remember going to one as a sophomore with two friends. We promised to stick together. But when the cops arrived to break up the party, my friends were nowhere to be found. I looked around. Not seeing anyone I knew, I panicked. So I ran.

By the time I stopped, I didn't know where I was. Everyone had scattered. I didn't have a cellphone, Google Maps, or a ride-sharing app, so I decided to walk. I figured I'd hit a main road and hail a taxi. I walked and walked, and I eventually made it to a roundabout. I stood at the edge of the traffic circle and waved for a taxi I hoped was driving by.

A light-colored sedan pulled over instead. A woman rolled down her window and asked if I was OK. She told me I was at the Maryland border; I had walked north instead of south. She was on her way home from synagogue and offered to drive me back to campus. Feeling scared, embarrassed, and ashamed, I decided to trust her, and she treated me with respect as she drove me to my dorm.

One blustery morning in late October, Maddie and I left my apartment for our regular walk around the neighborhood. Signs of the previous night's parties littered the ground. Beer cans, cigarette butts, and snack wrappers dotted the sidewalk and nearby grass.

Rounding the corner, I spotted a young woman in a short skirt and tank top. She was looking for something while desperately trying to stay warm. It was barely above freezing.

"Are you OK?" I asked, approaching her slowly. She looked at me with apprehension and panic.

"I can't find my car," she said, her eyes widening and her voice wavering. Her phone had died, she explained. She didn't know where she was.

"They probably towed it," I replied, and offered her my cell and to walk with her to my apartment building. The company's number was posted on a large sign by the door.

After she confirmed her car was towed, and without anyone to call for a ride, I requested an Uber and suggested we wait in my car, where it was warm. When I turned on the engine, a Christian song began to play.

"Are you Christian?" she asked. I said I was. She explained how she had gone to church but wasn't going anymore. I don't recall the specifics of the conversation, but I remember telling her she was always welcome. Her demeanor changed, and she smiled when we said goodbye. Somehow, I knew she could sense the love of Christ in our exchange. I could feel it, too.

I thought back to college and the Jewish woman, my angel in disguise, who found a lost and scared young woman looking for a ride and, recognizing the danger of the situation, offered to drive her safely back home.

Then I remembered the man who drove by a few moments after I met this young woman. My apartment was south of a neighborhood in transition. It had restored Victorian mansions; vacant, boarded-up buildings; and public housing. The man had called out inappropriately to the woman as we walked back to the apartment. I felt chills as I recognized, for the first time, the dangerous situation we were both in.

By helping this woman in her moment of need, I believe God gave me the gift of his perspective. He showed me my spiritual journey, one with clear bookends that measured my personal and spiritual growth. I was once someone in need, but now was someone who could help. I had transformed from someone ashamed and fearful of judgment to someone who could share God's love and grace.

Not all stories are journey stories, however. Over the years, I've identified four different types, or genres, of faith stories:

- **Miracle Stories** show God's ability, as the creator and healer, to interrupt scientific laws with divine intervention.

- **Valley Stories** share how God walks with us through grief, pain, or devastating circumstances.

- **Journey Stories** tell of God's transforming relationship as he takes us from one place to another. Sometimes literally, such as on a mission trip, or spiritually.

- **Mustard Seed Stories** show how God reveals big truths to us in the ordinary moments of life.

## MIRACLE STORIES

When a small-group leader recounted her testimony of attending a healing service and witnessing a miracle, I was skeptical. I was in my early 30s and living on the "Space Coast" of Florida. My churchgoing friends worked at NASA or in the space and defense industries. I was the only one with a liberal arts degree, yet I was the one who doubted.

I tried to wrap my mind around what she was saying, a devoted Christian whose husband was a self-described nerd in the Air Force. Wasn't it the scientists who didn't believe in God, the engineers who wanted proof before they believed?

She confessed her doubt as well. Before the service, she asked God to open her eyes and heart to the miraculous. That night, she saw a man with a distinct limp fully healed, and her heart changed.

I prayed a similar prayer years later after hearing about a miracle at the church I now attend in Iowa. While praying, a church member felt prompted to put a ring against the wall. Instead of falling, it remained suspended in air, as if the wall's paint had transformed into a glue strong enough to hold precious metal afloat.

Word spread and a woman I knew told me she witnessed the miracle as well. She invited me to her apartment and, after a while, she felt prompted to pray.

She put a ring flat against the wall. It should have fallen, but instead it stuck. I looked at it, mouth open in awe.

After a few seconds, she took the ring down. I put my fingers on the wall; it was paint and drywall. Smooth. Nothing that would cause it to stay. Then I inspected the ring, turning it over in my hands. It was like any other wedding ring.

Soon there were dozens of stories of rings sticking to walls. At one of the morning services, the senior pastor told the stories of the miracles circulating through the congregation. **A Miracle Story is when God does something outside the laws of our world as a blessing.** When I asked a different pastor about the ring, he reiterated it was a sign of God's love. A gift from our Heavenly Father.

I wanted to know more. What did it mean for me? I almost asked if he could interpret it — there must be some other meaning, I thought. Didn't God have something more specific for me, a clearer message of my purpose or calling? Or at least a specific next step I should take in my life? Then I noticed the weariness in my pastor's eyes.

Over the last few days, he had met with people who put a ring on their wall and saw the miracle, but more who prayed for a miracle and did not receive one. Their marriages were failing or they were suffering in another way, and they desperately wanted a sign from God. They fell on their knees. They asked humbly. Confidently. They placed a ring on the wall, desperately wanting it to stay. Instead, it fell.

I don't know why God gifts a miracle to one person but not another. Why is one child healed, but another isn't? When you share your miracle story, address this mystery directly. Say explicitly: I don't know why God chose to heal me and not someone else; why God selected me to witness this miracle but not another.

**By acknowledging the people in your audience who want a miracle but have not received one, you allow your story to be relevant.** You acknowledge their pain and still celebrate your joy. You also take away any implied hierarchy. We are equal in God's eyes, loved and cherished as children. Giving a gift to one child doesn't mean he or she is better than the other; it means one child received a gift from their Heavenly Father, and all good fathers give gifts to their children. The gifts just aren't all the same.

## PRAYER PROMPTS:

- God, where were you before, during, and after the miracle I experienced or saw?

- What do I need to know about the miracle?

- What truth did you reveal to me through this miracle?

- In what way do you want me to share this miracle with others?

## VALLEY STORIES

In my late 30s, I was hospitalized for a few days. It was a trying time, and fear overwhelmed me. When I opened the Gideon Bible one of the staff members gave me, I turned to Psalm 23:4 and found comfort in David's words: "Even though I walk through the darkest valley, I will fear no evil, for you are with me; your rod and your staff, they comfort me."

As I lay in the hospital bed, I prayed. God answered with the blessing of sleep.

Darkness is real. The battle is real. But God won the war. As Jesus said in John 16:33: "I have told you these things so that in me you may have peace. In this world, you will have trouble. But take heart! I have overcome the world."

**Valley Stories share how God walked with you through the trying times of your life.** They are agonizing, even excruciating, to live through. Yet they make gripping tales. The life-or-death stakes keep an audience on their toes, which is why Valley Stories are so often told in movies, books, or speeches.

But just because the entertainment, media, or publishing industries deem a specific type of story "worthy" doesn't mean the storyteller —

the one still living the story — is ready to share. Remember, you are the keeper of your story. Trauma. Grief. Life-changing events. It's not unusual to have a story you're still processing, still healing from, or not yet ready to share in a public or vulnerable way. You — not your friends or family or a well-meaning leader, but you the story keeper — decide if and when to share your story.

One challenge will be keeping your Valley Story short to meet our guardrails of 700 to 1,200 words or six to eight minutes in length. It's short for a reason; I've seen storytellers get lost in their story and lose control, creating an emotionally unsafe environment for them as well as their audience. It's as if a dam broke inside, and the water rushed forward, pouring out, unable to be rerouted or pulled back. It's a sign healing is still needed.

By embracing the constraints of word or time limits, you create a guardrail that keeps you and your audience safe. You focus on telling a full story, not a complete one; you select only the most revealing details instead of sharing all of them. And you refine and refine until you've polished the one main point you want your audience to remember.

Later, when you feel called to share your story in other ways, this boundary can be expanded based on the audience or format. You might share a one-minute version during a chance encounter, a five-minute version with a friend, or a 15- or 30-minute version if you're speaking to a group. You might expand it into a memoir or collection of short stories about your life.

**It's one of the mysteries of storytelling: To learn to tell a great story, you must start small.** The more limitations, the more intentional you must be. Authors master the short story format before graduating to a novel. Journalists write breaking news stories before they tackle in-depth, multiday series.

As you prepare your faith story, ask God what can be left out. Only include details that move the story forward. No "rabbit trails" or tangents that don't lead to your resolution.

Your first draft may have multiple points to your story, which is typical with Valley Stories. But multiple points will also confuse your audience. **Select one point, what we call the Story Anchor, to reveal at the end of your story.** Many storytellers make their Story Anchor one of

God's characteristics or truths, such as love or redemption. Others focus their story on a scripture, verse, Bible story, song, or hymn.

## PRAYER PROMPTS:

- God, how do you view my Valley Story?

- What details should I include in my story, and what details can be left unsaid or implied?

- How did you show me you were with me in the valley?

- What did you reveal about your nature as I walked through the valley?

- What Story Anchor do you want me to share?

## JOURNEY STORIES

In my late 20s, I worked in Oregon — before moving to Florida and eventually settling in Iowa — and I loved hiking the Coastal and Cascade mountain ranges. I was never brave enough (or crazy enough?) to climb a mountain that required special gear or equipment, but I was fascinated by those who did.

I read multiple biographies of professional mountain climbers who reached the world's tallest peaks. News reports focused on their ascent to the top and their achievement. Yet their memoirs spent only a few paragraphs on these moments. The rest of their books focused on the arduous task of becoming fit enough to climb and the long and dangerous journey to the summit and back.

I always imagined a long celebration after reaching a mountain peak, but while they enjoyed the view, the professionals didn't stay long. It wasn't safe or sustainable, and they knew they were only partway through their journey. They still needed to descend. It's why inexperienced climbers get into trouble, they explained. Too often, novice climbers prepare to summit the top, but they don't train for the climb down.

In the same way, **Journey Stories share how God takes us from one place to another, whether physically or spiritually.** Mission trips are typically Journey Stories, and they're sometimes described as "mountaintop experiences." I can see why. Away from the routine and comfort of home, you can see and experience God in new and profound ways. You anticipate and prepare for the journey. You scale a spiritual peak, but staying isn't sustainable. At some point, you must return home.

Luckily there's a storytelling model for us in Acts 11: "Starting from the beginning, Peter told them the whole story." By starting at the beginning, you take your audience with you, from preparing for a mission trip to spending time on location to your return with a changed perspective.

**While Journey Stories can be externally focused, such as a trip or career transition, they can also be internally oriented.** Internal journeys are often described as spiritual awakenings, conversions, or callings. The best stories have elements of both.

If your story involves shifting your beliefs to a true understanding of God — just as Isaac's classmates shifted their beliefs to an accurate understanding of his scars — add the qualifying phrase of "false belief." For example, "His classmates falsely believed his scars could catch fire." Or: "I falsely believed in a faraway God who didn't care about my life."

As you pray through your story, reflect on your audience. Ask God what he wants you to share, what details you can add, what descriptions you can tell. Enough for others to imagine themselves in your shoes. Your audience may never go on a similar journey, but they can relate to and experience the same gifts God gave you through your story.

## PRAYER PROMPTS:

- God, where were you on this journey with me?

- How did the journey change me emotionally, physically, or spiritually?

- What do I know now to be true about you, God, that I didn't before this journey began?

- How can I share this experience with the audience in a way they will understand?

## MUSTARD SEED STORIES

Early one morning, with my Bible across my lap, I sipped my coffee and found the verse where I left off the morning before. I was in my early

30s and slowly reading through the Psalms while sitting on my first piece of furniture not put together from a box.

It was the first time I made room in my life to explore my faith. I sat in the same spot every morning, read a few verses of scripture, and wrestled with God in prayer. I wanted to explore what I believed, what God said, and how the two aligned.

As I read Psalm 139, I let the words roll over me. Then I reached verses 13-14: "For you created my inmost being; you knit me together in my mother's womb. I praise you because I am fearfully and wonderfully made; your works are wonderful, I know that full well."

I stopped. Frustration swelled and then turned to anger. How could no one have told me? God loved me so much he created me to be — me? It went against everything I believed about myself at the time: The poor eyesight that meant wearing glasses since age 3. The body I wished was taller and thinner and a lot less clumsy. The mind I didn't think was smart or clever enough.

Yet there God was, showing me something others tried to tell me. How many times did my parents tell me they loved me? How often did teachers remind me of my value? The message was there, but I didn't hear it. Not until God spoke it to me through his Word.

My mind wandered back to the bullying I endured in middle school and the loneliness I felt after going a whole year without speaking to another student. I thought something was wrong with me, not the situation or the bullies, but me. The shame followed me when I transferred to a new school in eighth grade, and it accompanied me to college and into adulthood. I tried to shake it off for years.

I had pushed the memory into a hidden corner of my consciousness, where it simmered and stewed until it finally overflowed into that pre-dawn morning. Tears welled in my eyes. For the first time, I saw myself from God's perspective. How God created me the way I am for a reason; that I am lovable because he made me lovable; that I am loved because he loves me. As I cried, I felt the mountain of unworthiness come crumbling down on an ordinary, otherwise uneventful morning in the comfort of my new armchair.

**Mustard Seed Stories are small moments that grow into a big revelation about God.** In the Gospels, Jesus uses a mustard seed as a metaphor to explain faith. How the smallest seed grows tall and strong, larger than the other garden plants. In the same way, a Mustard Seed Story starts with an ordinary moment that grows into a significant truth about God.

**When someone tells me they don't have a story, it's often because they have a garden of Mustard Seed Stories.** Mustard seeds are the size of a sharpened pencil's tip. About five can fit on a pencil's eraser. I think about them when I plant lettuce, which is the tiniest seed in my garden. It's hard to see where I put them, as they blend into the black dirt of my raised bed. It's only after the lettuce sprouts that I know where they are. Mustard Seed Stories are similar as they can easily be missed, but once they are revealed, God's truth couldn't be clearer.

## PRAYER PROMPTS:

- God, where were you in an ordinary moment of my life?

- What stories from my past connect to this moment, and where were you then?

- How did this mustard seed of a story grow and blossom in my life?

- How did you use this mustard seed of faith to move a mountain in my life?

- What do I know to be true about you, God, that I didn't before?

## KEY CONCEPTS AND APPLICATION

- **God works in all things for good.** He doesn't cause bad things to happen but provides ways to offer redemption and grace. As you pray through your story, what anecdotes come to mind? How do the anecdotes connect to form a story with a beginning, a middle where something changes, and an ending that brings resolution and shares a deeper truth about God?

- **Miracle Stories share how God defied the laws governing this world,** whether by turning water into wine, healing the sick, or sticking a ring to a wall. They are blessings and gifts. As you share your story, acknowledge you don't know why you received a miracle and someone else did not.

- **Valley Stories share how God walked with you through challenging or devastating circumstances.** Remember, you are the keeper of your story. You decide how much to share, and whether you are ready to share with composure and self-control. Limit your story to one main point, or Story Anchor.

- **Journey Stories share a complex or challenging time and how God walked with you through it.** Start at the beginning and bring your audience through the whole story, from when you started the journey, through the physical and spiritual changes, to how it resolved when you returned home, whether physically or spiritually.

- **Mustard Seed Stories are tiny stories that reveal a big truth about God.** These include seemingly ordinary moments. Often, the revelations are spiritual. Allow God to show you what pieces of your story are connected to him and how his truth changed you.

CHAPTER 3
# YOUR STORY IS A GIFT

I pumped my legs back and forth on a swing set in our backyard in Minnesota, the summer breeze blowing my hair. My mom could see me from the kitchen window, and I could see her. Around my play area was a tall, thick fence my uncle built. Despite being 4 years old, inside the fence I was free to run and play.

It was a sunny day, the smell of cut grass lingering in the wind. Feeling adventurous, I climbed the stairs of the attached slide, positioned myself, and pushed off. I whizzed down and landed on a patch of dirt worn thin from my feet. Then I felt a sharp pain on my arm. Shocked, I screamed.

Hurt, confused, and surprised, I burst into tears, ran onto the deck, opened the sliding door, and hurled myself into my mother's arms. She held me, asked what happened, and concluded I slid into a bee.

My arm throbbed. I choked back tears, trying to make sense of what happened. I took a few deep breaths, my emotions a whirl. I was furious at that bee!

I don't recall what happened next. I likely played inside, apprehensive about the sting. But I loved being outside. I still do. Eventually, my desire to be in the sun and barefoot on the grass won over my hesitation.

This time, I was tentative. I walked to where I hit the bee and looked around. I didn't see it anywhere. The mix of grass and clover was the same. The slide and attached swings were the same. Yet something had changed. The world didn't seem as safe.

As I grew older, I occasionally thought back to the bee, my first and only sting. My mom doesn't remember, but it's etched in my memory as if it happened yesterday.

Eventually, I saw the humor in it. The bee was probably as shocked as I was. There it was, minding its own business above a nice patch of grass, when a red-headed girl slid right into it. The defended itself, lodged its stinger into my freckled skin, and died instantly, never knowing what hit it.

Over time, my mind connected the dots in the same way Isaac's classmates did. I formed a perspective of the world: It was random and dangerous. One moment I was happily playing outside and the next screaming in pain. The story I constructed aligned with my false belief that God was far away; that he set the world in motion and left us alone to fend for ourselves.

But was that actually what happened? I was a journalist, after all, and wasn't I trained to ask questions of everyone involved? I prayed through my memory and asked God to reveal his side. I closed my eyes and asked: God, where were you? Gently, I felt his answer: In the comfort of your mother's arms. A wave of peace washed over me. I knew it was true.

I'm not allergic to bees. I was never in mortal danger. When something went wrong, my mom was there. The whole story took only a few moments to unfold, and it could have been lost in my haze of forgotten childhood memories. Instead, it was preserved so one day I could know God's comfort is with me wherever I go.

**Before you write your story, ask God to share where he was in your story. Ask him questions in prayer.**

Focus on the "where" and "how." If God doesn't answer your "why" question, that's OK; I believe some questions are too big for us, in our limited knowledge and experience as humans, to know or understand. Like the children in Isaac's class, we might draw the wrong conclusion as we don't have all the information. Instead, investigate your story as a journalist by asking God humbly through prayer.

God answers prayers in many ways. Sometimes it's a deep sense of knowing. I joke that God lives in my gut, as my intuition has been refined during my years as a journalist, and I always regret not following it. Sometimes people hear a whisper or the voice of God. Others see pictures or images or movies with special meaning. Some like to journal while they pray, although that's not necessary. The key is to ask and then to listen.

## PRAYER PROMPTS:

- Where were you in my story?

- How did you reveal yourself to me?

- What do you want me to know about you, God?

## WE ALL HAVE MANY STORIES

My first memory, which I just shared, is a vivid story. But it's not my only one. There are many I could share: When I learned to pray as an elementary student. When I switched middle schools after being bullied.

A car accident in my late 20s, the years of pain, and a failed marriage engagement that left me wondering if I'd ever have a family. Moving to Iowa in my late 30s, meeting and marrying my husband despite the world shutting down during the pandemic of 2020, and becoming a wife and stepmother.

The Bible is our best example of a **Meta Story, or a collection of stories that make an overarching narrative.** Some Bible stories span chapters, some paragraphs, and others a single sentence. I think of the lineages in the Bible, a single name represents a lifetime. Each book, chapter, and story connects; the lineages serve a greater purpose than a simple chronology. Taken as a whole, it becomes the story of God creating us, redeeming us through Jesus, and reuniting with us in heaven.

**I am more than one story, just as you are.** Just as Jesus is. Each story in the Bible shows a different facet of Jesus: As a son, child, and friend. A teacher, a healer, a miracle worker. The son of Man. The son of God.

If you have a big story, one that feels overwhelming or that sets your life on a different trajectory than you imagined, it can be tempting to think it is your only story. That this one story defines who you are or how others perceive you.

That was my false belief, too. A car accident in my late 20s left me with herniated and bulging discs in my neck and back. The pain was always present, and doctor's appointments and therapy sessions were front of mind.

The emotional and spiritual struggles I'd pushed down were bubbling up and bursting through. My past hurt intertwined with my present pain, which confused and even angered me.

Why was my therapist asking about my family history, not my herniated discs? Why were we discussing boundaries, not managing my pain? And why was my world falling apart when I had thought, before the accident, I finally had it all together?

My injuries unleashed all my pain at once. The weight was unbearable. One evening, lying on my back on my bedroom floor, weeping so hard I could barely catch my breath, I knew I needed help. There was no more strength or will to pull from. I had reached the end of myself.

"I can't do this alone," I whispered that night to God. "I need your help."

I closed my eyes. I felt a warm and loving light come over me. A cloud of peace and strength engulfed me. I reached out to the God of my childhood, and he answered, not with words, but with a peace that dried my tears and quieted my mind.

God kept answering. Through a doctor who suggested I go to church, a couple who welcomed me to service, and a small group who met weekly to read and discuss the Bible. The physical pain and limitations didn't go away, and yet I began to heal.

A few years after the car accident, my neck and back still hurt, a dull pain I learned to brush to the corner of my mind. One Sunday, while visiting a different community's church. I sat in their tall, comfortable chairs that supported not just my back but my neck, giving me a momentary sense of relief.

The preacher talked about heaven, a place of God's love, a place without hurt or suffering. Tears streamed down my cheeks as I realized I would not always be in constant pain. If I wasn't healed in this lifetime, I would be in the next.

I wasn't physically healed in that moment, but in a spiritual sense I was. For the first time, I knew God was good. Despite the pain and physical injuries, despite the suffering I endured, I would one day be pain free.

## YOU DON'T HAVE TO SHARE IF YOU AREN'T READY

It took me seven years to share the story of my car accident. I was wrestling with physical limitations and anxiety and spiritual questions. It wasn't yet time to share my story, I didn't have enough perspective to see my story clearly. To stop asking God "Why?" and instead ask "What do you want me to know?"

**If you're in the middle of a challenging story, you may decide not to share it right now.** Maybe the emotions are raw, or you're still processing what happened. Perhaps you feel unresolved guilt or shame that needs to be addressed. It's normal to need time and space.

While coaching storytellers, I saw individuals share a story not out of love but out of a deep wound that wasn't yet healed. One woman told me a story "she never told anyone," a phrase I recognized as a possible sign of unprocessed hurt or shame. Decades earlier, she almost killed herself and her young child. As she recounted the events, she became emotionally wound up, and I could barely get a word in edgewise. She lost herself in the story and couldn't find a way out.

I interrupted her and encouraged her to talk to a counselor or a pastor. Someone who would receive her story and offer a path to healing and relief.

I knew if she shared her story in a public setting, it wouldn't be the storytelling experience she was likely seeking: affirmation, empathy, forgiveness. Nor would it be safe for the audience. They were expecting stories that challenged them, inspired them, but also entertained them.

Sometimes a storyteller seemed OK during practice but broke down onstage. I'll never forget a young man who told the story of his brother's suicide. He found his body and was wracked with guilt. He didn't know his brother was suffering.

As he told the story to hundreds in the audience, I started to tense. Around me, people shifted uncomfortably in their seats. Not because his story was challenging — we shared plenty of painful stories — but because he was using the public forum to make himself suffer even more.

I hate to use these words, but it started to feel like a self-inflicted lynching, a voluntary belittling or scapegoating. It took everything in me not to pull him from the stage and tell him: You are loved. You are worthy of healing. There are trained professionals who will guide you. It's not your fault.

That's been true for me. When I finally allowed myself to grieve — to feel the emotions I thought would overwhelm me — I started to heal. I finally understood what Jesus said in Matthew, "Blessed are those who mourn, for they will be comforted."

**If you are still healing from a story so raw it feels like yesterday, give yourself the gift of grief.** Even if it happened months, years, or decades ago, publicly sharing a story is not the first step to healing. The audience doesn't have the tools to comfort or guide you in your grieving process. Others do. A trusted friend, counselor, or pastor is a better place to start.

## TELLING CHALLENGING STORIES IN A 'PG' WAY

While I was babysitting one night, a preteen and I decided to watch a medical drama. I didn't think twice about the storyline. The doctors always seem to save the day, and he'd been fine watching epic movies about intergalactic battles with gruesome-looking bad guys and more hand-to-hand combat than I prefer.

But he woke with a nightmare after reimagining the episode's narrative, prompting his dad to express his concern. Embarrassed at my poor judgment, I apologized and promised to do better next time. Then I kicked myself for not picking a more age-appropriate show.

While the premise seemed far-fetched to me — a terrorist plot ripe for New York or D.C., not our small suburb in the Midwest — I also didn't grow up in an era of school shootings or airport security gates.

The television show was realistically told: It took place in a hospital, not a far-off galaxy. The fictionalized youth and my charge were the same age and gender, without superpowers or neon spandex to draw a clear distinction.

In retrospect, it was easy to see why his imagination got the best of him. He focused on the graphic display of sickness and imminent death instead of the show's celebration of hope after doctors rescued a young boy.

**When something deeply affects us, it becomes part of our story.** It may have been terrible, seemingly unspeakable. It happened. It's real. No matter how dark your story is, however, you can share it with any audience by focusing on the light. When you're at peace with your story, the dark details don't hold power over you. They are just the facts of what happened, and you can share those facts in a "PG" or "PG-13" way.

If you feel called to share a story of darkness and wouldn't want a student to hear the details, ask God to show you another way to tell your story. Just as a movie will allude to events without showing them directly, you can convey the essence without diving deep into past trauma or hardship. Instead of focusing on what happened, describe how it made you feel or how it influenced your life.

**A metaphor is a powerful way to share the impact of darkness while shifting your focus to God.** Think of metaphors as modern-day parables. Your audience will relate as they'll naturally substitute a story from their own life. You can turn to the Bible for examples. Take Matthew 7:27, which describes what happens to a house built on sand: "The rain came down, the streams rose, and the winds blew and beat against that house, and it fell with a great crash."

Remember, you are the keeper of your story. That means you are responsible for what you share and what is left unsaid. If your story disparages or harms another person, limit the detail and shift the focus to how you felt. Instead of describing how horrible an ex-spouse was, focus on how hurt you felt when your marriage ended in divorce.

Consider using a metaphor, such as the one used to describe pain and suffering in Isaiah 43, which also describes God's actions through it: "When you pass through the waters, I will be with you; and when you pass through the rivers, they will not sweep over you." The waves and storms came, the future was uncertain, but despite the unpredictable and dangerous currents, God kept you afloat. He was with you the entire time.

**Movie ratings can help you decide how many details to share** based on the audience you are sharing it with:

- If there are young children, a "G" story does not include darkness or violence. The main character is never in any real danger. Dark details are glossed over or shared in a metaphor a child would understand.

- In "PG" stories, a mention of darkness or violence could occur, but nothing intense. There's never a moment where you think the darkness will win.

- In "PG-13" stories, there may be more details about violence, strong language, or references to sexual situations or drug use. But it never contains adult material, intense or graphic scenes, or detailed descriptions of drug use or sexuality.

Why not include "R-rated" details? Because your story is a gift, and I want you to be able to share it with any audience. Keeping your story "PG" forces you to pay close attention to the story arc and how you structure your beginning, your middle where something changes, and your ending that brings resolution.

Graphic details can also override the meaning behind your faith story, drawing attention to the darkness instead of God's light. Stories that deal with an addiction, crime, ethical wrongdoing, or circumstances that condemn someone's character should be treated carefully.

**Unless there is a criminal conviction, no story should allege wrongdoing by including the allegation**. That's partly because the Faith Storytellers Framework teaches you to focus on your relationship with God, not your relationship with other people. But also because there can be legal consequences for defamatory statements or written allegations. I'm not an attorney, so you'll have to consult one on how the law applies to you.

If you are feeling the weight of a story about criminal wrongdoing, ask God if he is bringing it to mind in order to resolve the story, such as by seeking justice or granting forgiveness. You may need to take the next step to "finish" your story before you share it. Ask God for clarity about the direction to take, including whether to speak to a trusted friend, pastor, or law enforcement official.

Regardless of how dark your story may be, ask God to reveal where he was then and where he is now. Ask how he loved you then and ask how he shows his love now. Remember the promise God makes in John 16:33: "I have told you these things so that in me you may have peace. In this world you will have trouble. But take heart! I have overcome the world."

## STORIES ARE GIFTS

During one of our newspaper's storytelling events, I listened as a storyteller told a story I couldn't relate to. The details escape me, but I recall telling a friend it wasn't for me; it struck me as political grandstanding. All I could see was the storyteller's views, which were opposite of mine. As I coached her story, we butted heads over what to include and what to leave out.

A few weeks later, I ran into an older gentleman I knew. He had watched the storytelling night on local television, thanks to a partnership with a regional station, and couldn't wait to talk to me about it.

With tears in his eyes, he told me how much that same story resonated with him and how he better understood his own story because of it. He believed the story showed how much a father loved his son, a storyline he'd struggled with his whole life.

One story. Two interpretations. Evidence of the Holy Spirit at work.

Before you tell your story, ask God to use it in ways you could never imagine. Ask him to give you words that will resonate, to guide your story to the right person at the right time, and to make it available to those who need it most.

It's helpful to define what a story is and what it is not. **Stories are gifts given with love, an open heart, and without expecting something in return.** Like a Christmas gift, the joy comes in giving the story away.

In our culture, however, the definition of a story is no longer clear. A story, in its essence, has a beginning, a middle where something changes, and a resolution. A story includes stakes; something is at risk. And a story shows a transformation.

**A story is not a speech, a tribute, or a sales pitch. It's not advocating for a particular cause, policy, or way of thinking.** It's not a means to an end. I reinforced this point repeatedly with the storyteller I just mentioned, perhaps clouding my view after she cut pieces that told other people what to do, how to live, and what to believe.

These declarations create distance between the story giver and the story receiver, pushing them away or prompting them to tune out instead of inviting them to lean in. It was difficult for her; she saw herself as an advocate. But this wasn't a political forum or debate. It was a night of personal stories.

## KEY CONCEPTS AND APPLICATION

- **It's natural to draw conclusions from a story, but in doing so, you may miss how God was at work.** By inspecting your story as a journalist, asking God questions, and humbling yourself in prayer, you may see God reveal himself in a new or different way. Consider asking God: Where were you in my story?

- **We all have many stories.** On a sheet of paper, draw an arrow across the page pointing to the right. On the far left write "birth," somewhere in the middle write "Jesus" for when you came to believe in him, and on the far right add "heaven." Then ask God to reveal different stories about your life. Make a note of them in chronological order. Ask God: What story do you want me to share?

- **Storytelling is a gift shared freely with others, with no expectation of receiving anything in return.** That's opposed to stories shared with an outcome in mind, such as desiring sympathy from another person; seeking healing through therapy; advocating for changes to policy; or influencing the lifestyle or beliefs of others.

- **If your story includes darkness, it happened. It's real. It's just not the whole story.** Be careful not to defame someone's character, even if they hurt you. Use a metaphor to describe the details. Name your feelings, what you believed then, and what God revealed to you now.

- **You are the keeper of the story God gives you to tell.** That means you are responsible for what you share and what is left unsaid. Unless there is a criminal conviction, no story should allege wrongdoing. Consider using a metaphor and focus on how it affected you and how God worked through the situation.

CHAPTER 4

# UNCOVERING DIVINE DETAILS

As a sophomore in college, I attended a meeting of Washington, D.C., city officials to write an article for a journalism class. Walking into that large, stone building and seeing the community's leaders seated above me in their chamber was intimidating. I questioned whether I had what it took to be a journalist. I didn't believe in myself or my potential.

The city meeting began and ended without acknowledging the half dozen college students in the audience. I was relieved, but also nervous. What would I write? How would I compare to my classmates?

I returned to my dorm and reviewed my notes, determined to go the extra mile.

I reflected on the structure the story was to take: A journalistic outline called the inverted pyramid, which places the most critical facts first and relevant but less urgent details below. It was a decent article about a local issue, but I didn't have all the angles. I knew I was supposed to include as much detail as possible about the impact of the decision and interview people with different perspectives. So I called the local fire chief and left a message asking if I could interview him for my school assignment.

I must have called four or five times, leaving message after message. I became fixated on adding his side to my story. Then I read an article from the local weekly newspaper, which quoted him. Finally! I copied and pasted the quote into my document, relieved I now had the "full" story.

At the following class, my professor commented on our assignments, paused, and asked if the fire chief was at the meeting. I held my breath. Classmates looked at each other, confused. The chief had not attended. The professor moved on to the day's lesson, but I could feel my cheeks burning. In my rush to write the perfect story, I did not cite the source of the chief's quote, violating journalism and college ethics.

I returned to my dorm room, panic building inside. The narrative in my head bore down on me. Soon, I convinced myself I would be expelled from college for plagiarism. I didn't know what to do, so I called my father. After I unloaded what happened and my fears and worries, he said simply: "Why don't you go to your professor and tell him what happened? Just start at the beginning and tell him the whole story."

I looked up my professor's office hours, took a bus to his location, and then sat across from him. I stammered through what happened, my intention behind it, how sorry I was, and how I understood if he failed me.

He looked at me and thought for a moment.

"Are you Catholic?" he asked.

"Yes," I said, tilting my head in surprise.

Originally from England, my professor previously worked as a foreign correspondent for the BBC. He covered wars in Africa and foreign affairs for one of the most respected news organizations in the world. I'm not sure what went through his mind, but I can imagine how I looked to him: a freaked-out young Irish American convinced her journalism career was over before it began.

It was the first time I confessed to something I did wrong and asked for forgiveness. Sure, I went to confession as part of my Catholic upbringing and schooling. I told the priest I was mean to my brothers, which I was. I felt terrible, but only momentarily. They were mean to me, too. And I certainly wasn't scared of the consequences, as I was now.

"Rewrite the story and turn it in," the professor said. "I'm not going to fail you."

Relief crossed my shoulders. I fell short. I was wrong. And somehow, the punishment I was expecting was excused. I was forgiven.

I left his office and whispered: "Thank you, God."

I didn't tell my friends about the exchange, embarrassed by my shortcomings. And I didn't see Jesus in this story until I prayed through it, asking God to reveal himself to me.

Now, more than 20 years later, I see God at work in my first real experience with forgiveness and grace. I deserved a marked-down grade, if not a failed assignment. Instead, I received a second chance. Just as

Jesus, who died on the cross and took my sins so I could be forgiven, gave me a fresh start.

Sharing this story feels vulnerable. I know I'm not perfect. No one is. But I still cringe when I think what others might say about me. If somehow this acknowledgment of my past mistake might make the rest of my story as a journalist less meaningful or worthy.

As I prayed, I saw this story representing God's grace. I had owned my mistake and never made it again. Despite the shame I felt for years, I had a sense of peace. Through the storytelling process — and praying through this story as I wrote this chapter — I saw how God used it to reveal himself to me. I became comfortable enough to share it with you here.

As a journalist, whenever I wrote profiles about a notable person, it was easy to focus only on the achievement. So I always looked for a "wart" to take them off the pedestal and make them more relatable. Human. If a story sounds too good to be true, it typically is, so the audience doesn't believe or accept it. And no one likes to listen to someone go on and on about how wonderful their life is. It's the challenges we relate to, not the accolades.

**The more vulnerable you are in your story, the more relatable it is to others.** It allows your audience to understand their own story because, deep down, we are all flawed, and we all mess up. Sharing a wart can feel scary or uncomfortable, but it's also freeing. Just make sure you have peace about sharing it. A faith story shouldn't make you feel guilty or ashamed; it should feel redeeming and healing. We're imperfect people in relationship with imperfect people, but we have a perfect God.

## SHARING YOUR TESTIMONY, NOT TESTIMONIAL

I covered a variety of stories in my 14-year newspaper career but only a handful of court cases. I steered away from the criminal justice system. I didn't enjoy writing about violence and conflict, so I found a gentler beat: education. Conflict is part of life, however, and the court system is one way to find resolution. So when a Florida county sued its school district over closing schools, I was the reporter assigned to go.

In the courtroom, the judge sat at a tall, elevated desk like on television. To his left was a witness stand with an empty seat. In front of him were attorneys and the clients they represented.

During the proceedings, witnesses took an oath and were asked questions. Their answers were based on what they experienced or what they knew to be true as an expert. They were giving their testimony. They weren't asked to connect all the facts or draw a conclusion; that would be left to the judge in this particular case or a jury in a criminal case. Instead, they were asked to share their story as they personally experienced it.

**It's not an accident the word "testimony" also describes a personal encounter with God.** It's how the early church spread. Believers shared what they witnessed. How Jesus died on the cross, was buried for three days, and appeared to believers after rising from the grave.

Take the apostle Thomas, who was not with the other disciples when Jesus came to them as the risen Savior. Thomas didn't believe their story. The church nicknamed him "Doubting Thomas," which seems a little unfair, at least to me. I think Thomas simply wanted the same experience the other disciples had.

I also don't know why it took so long, but the book of John says a week passed before Jesus appeared to Thomas. When he did, Jesus invited Thomas to touch his hands. To feel where the nails were. Where the spear thrust into his side. In that moment, Jesus revealed himself to Thomas, and Thomas instantly knew it was God, saying to Jesus in John 20:28: "My Lord and My God!"

Because Jesus is a teacher and rabbi, he turned the moment into a lesson about God's kingdom. He says: "Because you have seen me, you have believed; blessed are those who have not seen and yet have believed."

The Faith Storytellers Framework teaches the same structure as Thomas' story. At the story's beginning, Jesus comes to the other disciplines, but Thomas doesn't believe their story. In the middle, Jesus appears to Thomas and invites him to touch his hands, which sparks a change in Thomas's heart. In the end, Thomas shares his beliefs about God and states his resolution: "My Lord and My God!"

The one difference is how the Faith Storytellers Framework approaches the ending. Instead of standing in as Jesus the teacher — and sharing a lesson about belief — as storytellers we end the story and allow the Holy Spirit to work.

If Thomas were telling this story using the Faith Storytellers Framework, he might end with a description of his revelation. He was overcome with a deep knowing. His doubt was washed away in an instant. Thomas might describe what he was doing with a few key details: Tears clouded his eyes. His legs gave way and he dropped to his knees. Still holding Jesus' hands, he said: "My Lord and My God."

If he retold the story, he would need to signal that his story was over. To friends standing close enough to read his body language, a simple pause would confirm it was over. But in front of a crowd — especially those too far away to see him clearly — he'd formalize his ending with a pause and a simple phrase: "Thank you."

He wouldn't belabor the point or spend another five minutes rehashing what happened. He would go out on the most powerful note possible and let his proclamation — that Jesus is God, that he saw and believed — hang over the audience as they breathed it in and digested it with the help of the Holy Spirit.

When you end a story in such a poignant way, it resonates. It echoes through the room or in the reader's mind. You create space between you, the storyteller, and your audience, the story receiver. In my experience, the shorter the ending, the more powerful the story.

Many storytellers want to add more than is needed at the end, which does the opposite and waters down the story's impact. There's a reason why movies spend two hours building up the plot with anticipation and tension before resolving it in less than five minutes. When your ending is short, you leave the audience near their peak, the satisfaction of the story's resolution still fresh in their mind.

I've also seen storytellers want to turn their stories into testimonials, which are different than testimonies. In a testimonial, you endorse a specific man-made construct: a program, a ministry, a book, a product, or a lesson. In society, we see testimonials everywhere. On billboards, while shopping, in fundraising appeals, or when talking to our neighbors about what they did last weekend.

The words are easy to confuse, yet the effect of each is distinct. A testimonial can bring someone through the doors. A testimony can bring someone to faith. My prayer for the church is to share fewer testimonials and more testimonies. To embrace storytelling as a means in and of itself, to surrender any alternate purpose, and to set aside time or space to tell true, first-person stories about an individual's relationship with God.

While I want believers to share their testimonies, I'm also concerned it's become synonymous with a "Road to Damascus" moment, which tells of a sudden, divine intervention that marks a turning point: from nonbelief to belief, from darkness to light.

Not every testimony has such a dramatic turn of events, nor can many Christians point to such a specific instance of change. Instead of limiting a faith story to this narrative arc, consider shifting the question: What do you know now about God that you didn't before? How did you sense God's presence, and what did that mean to you?

When you reframe the question, you realize that everyone has a faith story to tell.

## GOD CAN ANSWER THROUGH A STORY

While I was away at college, one of the churches in my hometown in Minnesota burned down. Looking out the school bus window each morning, I had memorized the church's A-frame construction and red door. It was a familiar and comforting sight. It was a different denomination than the one I practiced growing up, but it was still part of my community.

I followed the news reports closely, keenly aware of journalism's role in sharing what happened and how the story unfolded. Prosecutors charged three teens with arson. The 18- and 19-year-olds told officials that they "built and threw a Molotov cocktail at the church after a late-night party at a hotel," according to the Associated Press.

I struggled to comprehend why someone would do such a thing. They were around my age, and one was a member of the Episcopal church he torched. It didn't make any sense. The destruction was palpable. Photos of the damage showed a few beams barely standing. Later, the building was leveled to the ground.

That summer I interned at a local newspaper in Minnesota near my home, my first taste of being a "real" reporter. One of my first assignments was to interview the church pastor down the street, which opened its doors to the displaced congregation in their time of need. Their building held both denominations until the church could be rebuilt.

I asked the pastor about what had changed. They shifted their service schedule and painted their front door red, she said. But on closer inspection, I saw their changes as a sign of solidarity, a nod to the Episcopal tradition of a red front door, which was used in the early church as a symbol of sanctuary and protection, that all who entered were safe from persecution.

I didn't have the skills to explore the story more, although I longed to. I was still learning to conduct interviews, gather quotes, and write clearly and concisely, yet I was overflowing with questions. Some without clear answers, such as why God would allow one of his churches to burn and why someone would do such a destructive thing.

After graduating from college two years later, I took a job in Maryland. I was in a new city, a new state, and still learning the best route to the grocery store. My first week, I was told a Catholic Church had burned down in a small town nearby. My heart filled with sorrow for the church and its people. It was the same denomination I practiced at the time.

The fire was deemed an accident, but it was still devastating to the parish, and I wanted to write the story I couldn't years before. As a reporter, I was given access to places most people were not, and I walked through the rubble with men hired to clean it up. Inside, they described the blaze and pointed out items the fire left untouched.

A 100-year-old painting of the crucifixion survived. So did a statue of the Virgin Mary holding the baby Jesus. The fire consumed everything else, leaving only remnants of the walls intact. To many in the congregation, it was a sign of hope. That God was there in the midst of the destruction. Why else would he leave these two pieces of the church standing as if they were brand new?

The church's secretary told me their first Mass in a new location was a joyous yet somber celebration. Families she hadn't seen in years, who had fallen away from the weekly rhythm of Mass, had returned to worship.

Support poured in from Christians around the state, not just Catholics but others who knew how precious a church home is and how devastating its loss can be. "St. Peter's is my family," one woman told me as I covered the story. "As hard as it was, I wanted to be there."

The priest led his flock. He encouraged them to look past the ashes and toward the horizon. I quoted him as saying: "Someday, we will look back and say it really pulled people together, and look at what we were able to accomplish out of the ashes."

His message brought me a sense of peace. It answered a question still lingering after the church in my hometown burned down. This time, I understood. God doesn't cause bad things to happen. He hates suffering; he hates destruction. God loves us through challenges and heartache, and God sends help through his people.

## DIVINE DETAILS

While teaching the faith storytelling class at my church in Iowa, where I live now, I challenged the storytellers to look for the divine details in their stories. **Divine details reveal the small, seemingly coincidental ways God reveals himself to us.** As simple as a painted red door or as profound as a century-old painting untouched in a fiery blaze.

One student's story was particularly powerful, which I share in the next chapter. While still a child, Abbie lost her mother and two sisters in a car accident. Years later, as an adult, Abbie found the strength to find and reconnect with people who stopped at the scene of the accident to help. She attended my class to learn how to tell her story and how her story could help others.

Following the framework, she prayed through her story and asked God to reveal more to her. She recalled the lyrics to a hymn at the funeral, "It is well with my soul." At the time, the words grated against her. Overwhelmed with grief and anger, she wondered: How could I be well?

Years later, Abbie noticed the hymn again. The exact phrase is part of a song by MercyMe, which wrecked her each time she heard it. This time, "It is well with my soul" took on a different meaning. It seemed to be a sign of resolution, of God redeeming the tragedy as much as it could be.

Divine details are easy to overlook. You may not notice them until you reflect on your story.

In addition, one divine detail may not stand out until its pair arrives. I call these "bookend moments," as if God is holding up the story from both sides.

The hymns, for example, drew Abbie's attention at different times in her life. Yet she didn't see their true meaning until they were taken, complementing each other like a harmony complements a melody. A fulfillment of Jesus' promise in the Beatitudes in Matthew 5:4: "Blessed are those who mourn, for they will be comforted."

Bookends can offer a sense of resolution. More than mere coincidences, these bookends speak directly into our lives, such as when I wrestled with why someone my age in my community would burn down a church. I never brought that question to God in prayer or voiced it out loud to someone who could take that theological question on.

God still found a way to answer when a parish priest offered a harmonic call to focus on the horizon, not the rubble. Despite the moments being a few years and a thousand miles apart.

As you pray through your story, imagine taking one volume off the bookshelf of your life. Flip to a chapter, dust it off, and run your finger across its soft pages. Do you see any notes in the margin? Highlights or underlines from a divine author pointing you to a moment of love or tender care?

Where did your Heavenly Father hold out his hand, signaling for you to take it and gently motioning as if to ask: "When you're ready, I have something to show you. Let's turn around and see what's next."

With such a weighty story, Abbie's challenge was whittling it down to fit within our length guidelines. Ultimately, she did not include this detail in her story. But God has a funny way of making his story known, especially if we're willing to lean in a little.

A former journalism colleague was looking for stories, and I mentioned Abbie's as a possibility. Before writing, Courtney spent a decent amount of time getting to know Abbie and the families affected by the accident.

While I never asked Courtney what she believes about God, I could see his fingerprints in the story she wrote. His divine details are too good for a journalist to pass up, and as expected, the hymn made a prominent appearance (read the article at **faithstoryteller.org/resources**).

Abbie's story not only ran in our statewide newspaper, but Courtney later told me it was the most-read piece on USA Today's website that day. The right detail transformed a good story into a great one, and I'd argue, a faith one.

## EMBRACING YOUR STORYTELLING STYLE

Abbie came into my faith storytelling class with dozens and dozens of pages of notes, a box of firsthand material, and a heart to share a tragic story that left the room silent after she shared it. She had documented her story as she lived it, processing it through journaling. She felt ready to share the redemption she found through God.

As she told her story, the weight of her loss and God's love lingered in the air. I was awestruck at the weight of the burden she carried. And blown away by the clarity and freedom God provided as she processed the loss of her mother and sister in a faith-filled way.

A woman in the same class stared at a mostly blank piece of paper, hesitant. She was unsure if she had a story. It would never measure up to Abbie's, she said.

But how do you compare? Hers was a gentle Mustard Seed story of God's faithfulness. Abbie's was a Valley Story about a particularly traumatic chapter of her life.

God values each of us equally. And he values our stories the same way. Both women had stories that honored God, hearts that wanted to share God's love with others, and meaningful, personal stories that would resonate with anyone who listened.

They also had different storytelling styles. One started with too much material and the other too little; one would keep only the key moments while the other racked her memory for what to include.

Abbie was a "Story Carver." She'd journaled through the experience and had enough material for a memoir, let alone a short story. Yet she felt overwhelmed with how much she had to work with, as most Story Carvers do, and was unsure where to start.

Her classmate, meanwhile, was a "Story Builder." She naturally took the opposite approach, constructing her writing from the ground up.

Both Story Builders and Story Carvers construct their story, and both encounter moments that feel like work as they decide what parts of their story to keep or cut away.

Story Carvers, for example, may start with notebooks full of interesting tidbits and recollections to draw from — a seemingly desirable place to start — or pages and pages of writing. However, the abundance of material requires them to painfully cut away moments that don't align with their Story Anchor or main story point.

Story Builders, on the other hand, face the daunting blank page, unsure if they even have a story to share. They have to add to their story a little at a time, just as Story Carvers have to whittle down their story.

If you're unsure of your storytelling style or want advice on working within your storytelling strengths and guarding against your weaknesses, take the quiz "What's your storytelling style?" in the appendix or online at **faithstoryteller.org/resources**.

Your storytelling style may change based on the story, too. I'm typically a Story Carver. I like to gather all the information before I sit down to structure and write a story. But sometimes, a Mustard Seed story appears, and I have to remember to add more details to bring it to life. Like the time I was running along the Mississippi River in St. Cloud, Minnesota, where I lived and worked in my early 20s.

I didn't enjoy running in the winter, but this morning it was above 30 degrees and fresh snow covered the evergreen trees and clung to pine branches along the trail. It was still and peaceful. My pace was steady and strong, and I was in awe of the river's beauty. Then I saw a cardinal perched on a snow-covered branch, the river in the background, a soft light flickering through the clouds. It was beautiful. I stopped in my tracks, emotionally overwhelmed.

Over the years, when I've felt low or unloved, I've thought back to when the cardinal came into view. I was the only one to see it. The only one to appreciate it. It felt like a gift from God, a gift sent for no one else but me.

As I finalized my last edits for this book, I saw another cardinal in the woods on a walk near my home. As if God was saying: "Remember how you felt when you saw me along the Mississippi? How you felt my love so deeply and fully and completely? Remember that feeling today. I'm with you on this journey. I'm with your readers as they see how I've worked in the lives of others. And I'm with all those who decide to write and share their own faith story."

## KEY CONCEPTS AND APPLICATION

- **Stories, by their nature, reveal your vulnerability.** Audiences tend to reject stories that seem too perfect as untrustworthy. When you share a "wart," or a vulnerability, you allow the audience to relate to you as a human, not a pedestal.

- **Testimonies share personal experiences, facts, and encounters** in a courtroom or faith setting. Testimonials, meanwhile, don't focus on God. They focus on the benefits of a human organization, product, or service. A testimonial will bring someone through the doors, while a testimony can bring someone to faith.

- **Divine details can easily be overlooked but can be revealed through prayer.** These details may be tiny, but they point their way to God. If the details God reveals to you have meaning and align with God's love and grace, they are significant, no matter how small.

- **Everyone has a natural storytelling tendency as a Story Carver or a Story Builder.** Some start with a mountain of material and, as Story Carvers, must whittle pieces away until the narrative forms. Others start with a blank page and, as Story Builders, must construct the story from the ground up. Both are challenging, and one is not better than the other. Take the storytelling style quiz in the appendix or **faithstoryteller.org/resources.**

CHAPTER 5

# FINDING REDEMPTION AFTER A TRAGIC LOSS

### BY ABBIE KAMPMAN

Each June, I go through a tub of old newspaper articles. This bin is deemed my "Crash Box" and contains every article about the horrific drunk driving accident that took the lives of my mother, my two sisters, my mother's boyfriend, and one man in another vehicle.

My mother and Todd, her boyfriend, were drunk. They were at fault. I don't know if I've ever thoroughly read the articles; I've infrequently skimmed them, then shoved the pile back in the box, too overwhelmed to absorb the words. I've done this over and over for the past 18 years.

Open, skim, shove, pack away again. It's almost as though opening that box is my Pandora. I don't want to allow the onslaught of emotions to hit me. But this time, I pulled it down from the storage shelf, pried off the lid, and pulled out the top article.

For the first time in nearly two decades, I fully absorbed the names: Lauren, Amanda, Samantha, Stephan, Josh, and Trooper Van Otterloo. I read each name, allowing my mom's face to appear, then Amanda's, then Sammy's. When I got to the other names, I realized I couldn't picture who they were. I wanted to. I was overcome with a need for more.

I absorbed the article's contents. I saw their names and remembered the story, lingering on each detail. The accident was 18 years ago, and now I was finally able to consider these families, their stories intertwined with my own. A realization hit me. The Internet. Facebook. I can find them. Do I want to know theirs? Would they want to know me, know my story?

## DISCOVERING MORE OF THE STORY

It took me an hour to find them. There were two I prayed would respond. Carla, the widow of the man who died in the other vehicle, and Josh, the faithful Good Samaritan who tried to get my mom and her boyfriend to turn around. Finding Josh proved more difficult than finding Carla, but I was certain I had found his wife. I messaged both: "You don't know me, but my name is Abbie Kampman …"

I explained who I was, that I was deeply sorry for the pain my family had caused, and that I hoped to hear back from them. Finishing, I paused, hesitating for a split second. Before I could rethink the decision, I hit send.

Now the waiting. I didn't expect to hear back. I assumed each message would rest in their spam folders, forgotten.

Three days later, a message popped up in my Facebook inbox from Stephan's widow: "Wow. I'm blown away. Yes, I am Carla. You found the right person. I'm so glad you decided to message me. Just wow. So many emotions, but mostly admiration for you. I am so sorry too. If you ever want to hear my story, I would happily share it. If you'd like to share yours, I'd love to hear about your sisters too. Thank you, Abbie. You are now always in my prayers."

My breath caught in my throat. She not only responded, but she seemed kind, generous, and forgiving. My body shook, overwhelmed by the magnitude of what just happened.

From that moment, the summer snowballed into a series of connections. I called Carla. We talked for over an hour. I contacted Josh, the man who drove alongside my mom's car. I connected with Steve, the state trooper who investigated the accident.

Each of these individuals provided comfort, peace, care, and generosity. God began to dress wounds that had never fully healed. He began to lift the weight from my shoulders. He began freeing the chains I didn't realize were holding me back for many years.

I began to search for anything I could find that may provide closure. In a conversation with Steve, he mentioned he could get me a copy of the accident report and photos of the bodies. I hesitated but said yes. I wanted no stone unturned.

I sent a request for the accident report per Steve's instructions. I asked for the photos. Many families of fatalities and homicides don't want to see them, but I did. I never got to see Mom before she was cremated. If I couldn't see her final brokenness, I couldn't think of her as anything but fabricated, untouched, and unharmed by her choices.

I needed to see the devastation that came from her hand. Her body, my sisters' bodies, Todd's, Steve's, the mangled cars, the debris, the wreckage that became her life. I needed to see how far I'd come since God had picked up the pieces. Mom left this earth with a broken body and, in turn, left me with a broken soul.

After dropping the request in the mail, I took a shaky breath. It's coming. Every detail I've ever avoided is coming. "Lord, be near," I prayed.

A few weeks later, the file arrived in a yellow manila envelope. I put it down for a bit, the contents too violent to handle. It was all too much. I wandered around the house, picking up toys, putting away books, and reading emails without actually taking in the information. Should I open it? I kept walking toward the envelope, then away. Finally, I picked it up, wanting to get it over with.

I sat down. Undid the metal clasp. Pulled out the papers. Department of Public Safety. Iowa State Patrol. File number 99-133. Hands trembling, I noticed a sticky note attached to the top paper. "The photos are coming. They are negatives and need to be processed at a separate facility. I will get them to you as soon as possible."

I exhaled.

Well, at least I can prepare myself further for those, I thought, slightly disappointed but knowing God has a reason for the delay; I needed to digest it in small bits. Too much. It was all too much.

I flipped the bound file to the first page and read through each word.

Page after page of technical details, what time the accident occurred, at which mile marker, how fast the cars were going, where they hit, at what angle they rested, and how much alcohol was in Todd's blood.

The reports seemed to focus on the drivers and the injured. My mother and sisters were left out of the technical details, their only representation in the final death count. Five. Five deaths. Where were their injuries, their ages, their lives, their stories?

Nothing. The only mention of them came at the end of the report, in the witness accounts. There were six statements, two from the surviving injured men in the other vehicle and four from bystanders who stopped to help. Josh's statement was in there, but the one that caught my eye was a woman named Lynne.

"We were heading home on Highway 218," Lynne had said. "I was watching the road ahead and saw dust flying. I told Wayne to stop. He pulled over right away, and our headlights shone on a child's body. We immediately got out to help and ended up pulling out another child, a little girl, from the wrecked car before it started to burn."

Lynne and Wayne. The couple who pulled Amanda from the car. They saw Sammy's body on the road. They were there; they touched their lifeless little arms, felt their hair, and probably had my sisters' blood on their hands and clothes.

I dropped the report. Too much. It was too much. Tears running down my face, I pictured Lynne driving along the road, the sun nearly gone on the horizon. The Iowa countryside flying by. Their car cresting the hill on Highway 218, the commotion ahead. Lynne urging Wayne to pull over.

Wayne steering their car onto the left shoulder, the car screeching to a halt, headlights still on. Following the beams of light and seeing a girl lying in the road. Her bleach-blonde hair and tanned skin covered in dust and blood. Lifeless.

Lynne jumping out, Wayne right behind her. Running to Sammy, feeling her pulse. Nothing.

Running to the car, dodging glass and mangled steel in the road. The smell of blood, exhaust, gasoline, alcohol. Another girl in the car's back seat, darker blonde, slightly older. Lifeless.

Prying the door open, pulling the thin body out before the flames overtook the front hood. Frantically trying to help two adults in the front seats but unable to pull them out, their bodies crushed and the flames licking closer.

I stopped. Too much. It was too much.

## SURRENDERING MY STORY TO GOD

These were my sisters, my mother, my family, my heart. I refocused my mind, tried to think of them as everyone else does when reading a newspaper article or watching the news. As a mere number, a death count. I couldn't.

That precious blonde preschooler, lying in the road, was seen by God. The thin, tanned 7-year-old — pulled from the mangled vehicle — was created in his image. The inebriated woman, crushed by the swiftly burning mangled vehicle, was dearly loved by her maker, the creator of the universe. These girls, women, were loved by Jesus, who wept at their brokenness. The same Jesus who wept with me.

For the first time in 18 years, I sobbed with grief over each of the souls that perished, feeling the full weight of love God has for each of his children. The love God has for me. I praised him for allowing me to meet the victim's family and witnesses. For the redemption of sharing our stories with each other and finding new relationships in the midst of our loss.

At that moment, I handed my burden over and acutely felt Jesus carry the weight away, taking it upon himself. I felt his love envelop me, and the chains of brokenness shattered.

I felt the walls around my heart crumble. I was finally free.

CHAPTER 6

# FAITH STORYTELLERS FRAMEWORK

Are you ready to write your faith story? I explain the Faith Storytellers Framework below with guidance on each step. As you walk through this process, remember God is with you, gently leading you through each step.

Don't try to rush the story-crafting process. I've benefited from taking short breaks or stepping away from the process for a few hours or days. You'll pick your story up with a renewed sense of purpose and fresh perspective.

A reasonable amount of time and space allows you to reflect on the constraints of the particular step in the framework and how it affects the story you write. This gentle approach creates an environment suitable for crafting meaningful and compelling stories that reflect the deeper truths of our beliefs.

## STEP 1:
### PRAY FOR GUIDANCE ON WHAT STORY TO SHARE

Like a sculptor deciding what image to reflect in clay, decide which of your many stories to share. Ask God what story he wants you to tell, which may be different from the story you first thought of when you picked up this book. We all have many stories, and he may have a particular reason for asking you to share a specific story.

As you pray, remember God answers in different ways. Sometimes people hear a whisper, see images or movies, or feel a deep sense of knowing. Whenever you hear from God, you can check it against Scripture to see if it aligns with the Bible. God will never contradict himself. As a journalist, I was schooled to question everything, and as a reminder colleagues would say, "If your mother says she loves you, check it out." The same holds true here.

## PRAYER PROMPT:

God, you gave me the gift of my story, which I know can bless others. You've also given me countless stories I can share. I ask you to reveal what story you'd like me to tell. I surrender the story selection to you, as I know you can and do work in all ways and in all things for good.

## STEP 2:
## DIVIDE YOUR STORY INTO THREE PARTS

Like a sculptor who first forms the head and shoulders, as a storyteller, you'll identify the main pieces of your story before adding specific details. Outline your story into three scenes and your Story Anchor, which is the North Star of your story, the main point that your three scenes will align with and lead your readers to.

In faith storytelling, your Story Anchor is a truth about God that you discovered and more deeply believed by the end of your story. This also means you didn't see or know or apply this truth at your story's beginning. The story arc — your personal transformation — comes from starting without this truth and ending knowing it.

By anchoring your story to a facet of God's character — love, compassion, service, relationship, or forgiveness, to name a few — you can be confident your story will honor God and reflect his light to others.

A faith story doesn't need to quote Scripture or refer to a Bible story. At its root, a faith story is a series of encounters or events that prompt us to wrestle with our spiritual beliefs until we adopt them as our own.

To discover your Story Anchor, reflect on your three scenes and how your convictions changed from beginning to end. Try completing this sentence: "What I know to be true about God that I didn't before is …"

**Scene 1:** The beginning of your story.

**Scene 2:** The middle where something changes.

**Scene 3:** The ending that brings resolution.

**Story Anchor:** One sentence that shares what you know to be true about God.

If you hated writing outlines in school, hear me out. This step's purpose is to shape the contours of your story. Some people write to determine what they want to say, others think or speak it out loud as a way of forming their thoughts. That's fine.

Just don't skip this step. You still need to shape and focus your story.

Some storytellers write their outlines from top to bottom. Others create a timeline from left to right. Or they draw a mind map by listing one idea in the center of a page and related ideas around it. They want to see all the possibilities before they select one.

The goal is to identify three scenes that reflect different moments of your spiritual growth, which you'll summarize in your Story Anchor. Each scene serves a different purpose for your audience: to show your life before your transformation, as you struggle to change, and after you cement your new belief or perspective into your life.

Some outlines are straightforward and have clear beginnings and ends. Take a weeklong mission trip. The story will start before the trip, transition to a particular challenge or struggle you faced during the mission, and conclude with how you integrated your new perspective into your "normal" life back home.

Other outlines are challenging to create and, in my experience, the most difficult part of crafting a story. You may know your story's middle, for example. The death of a loved one. A failed promotion. A cancer diagnosis. All moments that changed you — but how?

One approach is to work backward through your story. Identify your resolution, then an earlier moment when you believed the opposite.

It's a time-tested strategy, and why one of my friends hates dog movies. He recognizes the pattern: If the film starts with a playful and affectionate puppy, he knows this beloved pal will pass away near the end. He won't admit it publicly, but this friend told me privately: He doesn't want to cry during a movie.

But suppose the first scene shows an abandoned, pitiful-looking dog. My friend will agree to see it because he knows what to expect:

embarrassing and hilarious mishaps. The awkwardness continues until the reluctant dog owner decides this misfit of a mutt is "his," regardless of the consequences, and they drive off into the sunset in pursuit of their next adventure as best friends.

There are two common pitfalls at this stage of the story-crafting process.

One is mistaking any writing you did before your outline as your first draft. If you don't organize your story, you'll lose your reader before you begin. They won't be able to follow your meandering thoughts or long-winded descriptions, and they won't understand how the various anecdotes you've included relate to each other.

The second is more challenging to diagnose. It's when your three scenes don't align. Your beginning doesn't make sense with your ending, or your middle doesn't reflect the struggle you resolved in your resolution.

If you run into this issue, you may need outside help. Someone who can review your story to see where you went off course. This is the role editors play for writers: They stand in the reader's shoes and inspect your story for misalignment and unanswered questions. Without an editor, the next best option is to ask one (or a few) readers.

## PRAYER PROMPT:

God, you work in all things for good. You are good. You are love. And you love me. I ask you to reveal the pieces of my story you want me to include, and to trust the rest of my story with you for another time. Lord, grant me insight into my story's outline — the three parts of my story that show change — and the Story Anchor you want me to give as a gift to others.

## STEP 3:
## CREATE A NARRATIVE SEQUENCE IN EACH SCENE

Like a sculptor ready to craft unique features such as the nose or eyes, you'll start adding the moments that make your story unique. You'll add the following three pieces to each scene — the description and context of where you were, the action of what happened, and how you reacted. This is often called structural editing, since you work through what information to include and the order of each scene.

**1. Description.** Similar to a television show, which might flash to a picture of a house before cutting to the scene inside, the description allows the audience to quickly understand where the story takes place. You only need one sentence with two critical elements:
**A) Place.** Name where you were and what it looked like around you.
**B) Time.** Describe when it happened, such as how old you were, or the context of when it happened in your life, such as being newly married.

**2. Action.** Describe what happened that moves the plot forward. Include what's at stake. For example, your boss just approved an extended absence so you could volunteer with a mission in Africa when a mission leader calls and asks you to come a few weeks early. They could use your skills setting up a school. As the leader explains the situation, you realize it means time away from your family as well as your career. You'd have to forfeit a project that could lead to a promotion.

**3. Reaction.** Name how you felt. Your audience quickly identifies with your feelings, making your story relatable. For example, you may feel shocked at the leader's request to extend a mission trip, or outraged they would ask on such short notice. Or perhaps your excitement for the trip fades to apprehension as you consider what to do.

Sometimes, storytellers don't want to name their feelings, but it's a critical part of the short story format, as there's not time to fully express those feelings another way. If you don't know what you were feeling in the moment, that's normal. Just say it outright: "It was such a blur, I didn't know what I was feeling or how I should respond, but I promised to pray about it with my wife. I just didn't know what else to say at the time."

**Add your key detail.** After you've written these three elements of a scene, go back and ensure you have one key detail, which is typically one of your five senses. By mentioning how something sounded,

felt, looked, smelled, or tasted, your audience will imagine being
in your shoes.

- What you heard (the tires screeched to a halt)
- What you saw (the sunlight bounced off the snow)
- What you touched (the cold, hard stone beneath my bare feet)
- What you smelled (the smell of smoke lingered in the breeze)
- What you tasted (the salt in the ocean air)

**Repeat this process for the rest of the scenes.** Each of your
three scenes will follow this same structure: description, action,
reaction. Each scene will have one key detail.

**Refine your Story Anchor at the end.** It should describe what
you know about God that you didn't before. Be careful to stay in the
first person. It's easy to slip into teaching or preaching by adding
"you" or "your." Or to assume common belief with "we" or "our." If
you did — it's hard not to — that's OK. Just change it!

### PRAYER PROMPT:

God, you know my story better than I do. You also know how much
this story can bless others. I ask that you reveal what to include in each
scene of my story. What action should I incorporate? What reaction did
I have, if I'm being honest and vulnerable? What details help make the
scene feel real? Show me how to align each scene with your Story Anchor.
Give me the gift of one powerful sentence to end my story.

### STEP 4:
### REFINE YOUR STORY AND ADD DIVINE DETAILS

Like a sculptor adding the small details to make a piece come alive,
now is the time to refine your story. You'll carve the soft lines of hair or
add the gentle curve of a cheekbone.

You'll also edit your story for grammar, spelling, word usage, and
punctuation. But don't stop there. This is also the time to review every
sentence and paragraph to maximize its impact.

- **Look for divine details.** These are little moments or signs that have special meaning. Ask God to reveal his fingerprints in your life. Often, they are simple — a bird, a hymn, a chance conversation. As you look at these details, add them into your story in the order they appeared. You don't have to verbalize how these details are connected by saying, "Look at how these two hymns were both in my life!" Just include the hymn in each context, and then share what they meant to you at different times in your life.

- **Review your story line by line.** Read your story out loud, word for word, not just silently to yourself. You'll hear words or phrases that need to be changed. Split long sentences into two, as shorter is often clearer and easier for an audience to understand. In addition, make sure dialogue moves the story forward. Skip standard greetings or small talk ("Hey! How are you?" "Good, How are you?" "Fine. Did you see the game last night?").

  - **Story Carvers** will need to cut phrases, words, or sentences that are unnecessary or implied. Check your word count. It should be fewer than 1,200 words. Be ruthless! I often find myself, as a Story Carver, chopping whole paragraphs or "throat clearing" sections that served as a writing warmup or cooldown, but don't fit the story itself. Watch for "rabbit trails" that divert time and attention away from your Story Anchor.

  - **Story Builders** will need to do the opposite, and aim for more than 700 words. Find an isolated sentence and start adding sentences to its left or right. You'll want a clear path from one scene to the next, almost like steppingstones the reader or listener can follow as they move through your story. Think of details that will help your reader or listener imagine it, such as what they might hear, smell, taste, touch, or see.

- **Review your transitions.** By their nature, stories jump in time, and it will confuse readers or listeners if they lose their place in your story. Ensure every scene describes where you are and a time reference that creates context. Are you in your 20s, newly married with a baby on the way; or in your 20s, single, and moving to a new city for your first professional job? These can be short, a sentence or two at most. Think of a movie flashing an aerial view of a city before cutting to the action. It might write out the city's name and year to make sure the audience knows the story jumped to a different location and time.

- **Reflect on how you knew it was God.** In my experience, this is a question your audience wants answered, even if they don't ask. Consider your five senses and describe your experience with God as if you were explaining it to an 8-year-old. As you pray through your story, ask God to reveal how he showed himself to you.

- **Consider the tenses and verbs you are using.** The most powerful stories are shared in the present tense, as if you are experiencing your story for the first time, although past tense can be appropriate too. As much as possible, power up your verbs with action: run, act, wait, see, connect, cry, shout, lift, walk, sing. If your verbs are action-oriented, your story will flow more smoothly.

- **Never share information you wouldn't have known at the time.** If you're asking God why you haven't gotten married yet at age 30, don't tell us you'll get married 10 years later. Wait until you get to that part of the story. Allow tension to exist, even if it's uncomfortable, because it's part of life. Chances are, your audience is living with similar uncertainty and can relate.

- **Allow tension to exist, even if it's uncomfortable — especially if it's uncomfortable.** Tension in a story means something is at stake, which means something important could be lost. As the tension builds, your audience will lean in, and when your story finally resolves, your audience will sit back in awe. The greater the tension, the greater the release, the greater your resolution's satisfaction.

### PRAYER PROMPT:

God, you knew my story before it happened and were with me as it unfolded. As I walk through this editing and revising process, allow me to see my story from the audience's perspective. Help me see your fingerprints on my story, and the divine details you gave me to share. Guide me as I comb through each sentence to straighten out words and phrases, replace tangles with clear thoughts, and questions with answers. Walk with me in these small but necessary decisions, and give me peace as I make this story the beautiful gift you know it can be.

### STEP 5:
### PREPARE YOUR STORY TO SHARE

Like a sculptor who wants to prepare their creation for a live viewing, you'll polish your story and double-check that it aligns with the Faith Storytellers Guardrails. It's time to make your story shine.

- **Confirm you've met the Faith Storytelling Guardrails listed below.** Pay special attention if your story includes other people or denominations; faith storytelling is about uniting the church by focusing on God, not dividing it by sharing stories that might be perceived as condemnation or criticism.

- **Check your length. Are you within 700 to 1,200 words when written, or six to eight minutes when spoken out loud?** If you are speaking your story and haven't used a timer yet, do it now.

- **If you plan on speaking your story, practice telling it out loud from memory.** Don't rely on written words, and don't try to memorize it like a script, as you'll stumble when you share it (I've seen it happen too many times). By sharing from memory, you accept that you'll tell your story differently each time, but you'll always hit the main points. Your presence will be more robust, and you'll naturally share your story with more authority.

- **Share your story with another, trusted person.** Tell them in advance what feedback you want. If you're speaking your story, share it from memory. It's good practice and will help work out your nerves.

## PRAYER PROMPT:

God, you know how much this story means to me and how much it can help others. Please help me give my story as a gift, without expectation of return. Let me see where my story needs polishing so it can be received as the gift it is meant to be. As I practice speaking the story out loud, help me learn it by heart so I can always be ready to share it. Help me trust my story will resonate in the way you intend.

## KEY CONCEPTS AND APPLICATION

- **Pray about what story to tell.** After the first session of my faith storytelling class, there was always a handful of storytellers who decided to tell a different story.

- **Take breaks between each step of the Faith Storytellers Framework.** Our unconscious mind will work while we're away from our story. Take a brisk walk, get a good night's sleep, and return to it a day or more later.

- **Write or talk about your story to understand it before ordering it into an outline.** Complex, meaningful, and layered stories can benefit from this additional step. Getting your story out of your head and into an external form, whether a conversation or a written page, allows you to reflect on your experiences from an outside perspective.

- **Review your Story Anchor.** Does it fit into the three scenes you selected, or do they draw a different conclusion? If that's the case, consider changing a scene or switching your anchor or main point. We each have many points we could make about our stories. The challenge is limiting yourself to one.

- **Check your story against the Faith Story Guardrails, which protect yourself, your loved ones, and your audience.** Is your story PG or PG-13? Have you replaced the dark details with a metaphor? Use the quick reference in the appendix or visit **faithstoryteller.org/resources**.

CHAPTER 7

# SHARING YOUR FAITH STORY: A CONVERSATION WITH PAT JACOBS

Pat Jacobs came with her husband, Mark, to one of my faith storytelling classes to better understand how to share her story. Their oldest son had died in a plane crash many years before. Pat wrestled through her grief, and while it had never entirely left, she felt ready to tell her story. As a natural Story Carver, the challenge was length — it took 90 minutes to tell it! Two church staff members suggested the class, which taught the structure of storytelling and gave Pat a sense of agency over her story.

It's a powerful one. Before the crash, their son Eric had a dream he might die early. He woke up in the middle of the night and felt an urgency from the Holy Spirit to record a video. At first, he jokes about it. It seemed a weird thing to do, to wake up and record a video. But later, he starts to cry and leaves specific messages for his family.

I don't want to give too much away; you can read her story and many others in Part II of this book. We've also included a link to the video Pat mentions, which you'll find later in this chapter.

When I asked Pat about the class, four years had passed since she took the class. Parts of our conversation are below. It's incredible to see how God is working through her story. It doesn't take the pain or the heartache away, but as you'll see, God keeps opening the door for her story to be shared.

Before we hugged goodbye, Pat asked how I shared my faith with our boys, ages 11 and 16. It was a question echoing in my mind at dinner later that night when our oldest shared his concerns about his first part-time job. I didn't tell him what to do. Instead, I asked how he might handle his situation and shared stories from my own high school job, creating empathy and understanding.

He kept chatting with me, which I enjoyed, and the conversation continued well past cleaning up the kitchen and putting away the dishes. He shared the entire plot of his two favorite fantasy books, as a new book by the author was coming out. Then the conversation took a turn, and he talked about the real issue on his mind. When it rose to the top, I shifted the conversation seamlessly to faith.

When you share a story, you often receive a story back. To be a great storyteller, you must also be a great listener. As one of our pastors says, "Corn talk is important talk." In the agriculture community where he first served, farmers would talk at length about their corn before turning the conversation to what was on their minds. Corn. Football. Weather. Fantasy books.

Whatever the topic, small talk serves a purpose: to assess whether it's a safe or appropriate time to share the real issue and whether it will be received well.

Once you tell your story, it becomes easier to retell. A storyteller, once hesitant to tell their story out loud, gains confidence and conviction. Many go on to share their story bravely and widely with others.

Think of the Gospel story about the woman at the well. The Samaritan woman had an incredible encounter with Jesus and believed he was the Messiah. Amazed at what she discovered, the woman returned to town and shared her story with those who rejected her. She went from avoiding her neighbors to seeking them out. A true faith storyteller!

In John 4:39, her story became a gift to those who mistreated her — and the start of their own story of faith in Jesus: "Many of the Samaritans from that town believed in him because of the woman's testimony."

The townspeople wanted to meet Jesus and invited him to stay, and he did, for two days. Because of her willingness to share her story, her village came to know Jesus. They ate together and talked. In John 4:42, the townspeople told the woman: "We no longer believe just because of what you said; now we have heard for ourselves, and we know that this man really is the Savior of the world."

It doesn't matter how seemingly big or small your story, how painful or uplifting the circumstances. Just like the woman at the well's story, and just like Pat's, God can use your story as an invitation to know him.

## A CONVERSATION WITH PAT JACOBS

### What was it like to go through the Faith Storytellers class?

Kind of scary. (Laughs.) During the class, I realized I would have to speak without notes. That was intimidating! It was like having my crutch taken away. I know my story in and out and a hundred different ways, but it was like stepping out in the "Indiana Jones" movie, and there's no bridge. You must take that first step. And when you do, oh my gosh, it's going to work! The class helped build the bridge.

### What was your takeaway from the class?

It was a gift to explore different concepts in telling a story, which made it so much easier to tell because I identified a beginning, a middle, and an ending. I love how you start at the beginning, and then you take your story to a place with a beautiful ending, which is so revealing. It's how a story should end. And also being able to tell it in different increments of time. After the class, I developed a shorter version and then a longer version where I could really get into it.

### What did learning to tell your story mean to you?

How important it is for each of us to identify what our gifts are and what our story is. I'm an eight on the Enneagram (the personality test). I'm bold. I'm in your face. I take charge of situations without being asked. (Laughs.) Sometimes I can be overbearing, which is one of the drawbacks. I think Peter is an eight. He's the rock that built the church.

I look at it as my job to share my faith with whoever might ask, and I know it's the Holy Spirit who makes the opportunity available. It's a privilege and honor, and scary at times. I don't want to mess it up. (Laughs.) But the joy that comes from sharing my story overtakes the fear.

## What do you mean?

When I share my story, my goal is to say: What is it God's trying to reveal through me? Every single thing on this earth, whether it's a person, tree, leaf, or butterfly, manifests the face of God. We have such a unique opportunity to reflect God in our life. If Eric hadn't done his video, I wouldn't have had the opportunity to have this conversation. One little video represents an amazing opportunity. To ask and share: How is God reflected in my life? What is my story?

## And you have many stories.

Many, many stories. In fact, when I do my daily devotions, the verses trip my memories, and I relate it to one of my stories. I have never been disappointed. God has given me so many stories. It's exponential. I think this is exactly the joy God must have in watching each of us: Look what we are going to do today! Isn't this amazing?

## Let's talk about the class for a moment. What was the benefit?

Writing my story out made it very intentional, and it limited what I shared. I think that's what scared me. I couldn't just free-flow it. But that's what made it too long.

## You did a great job at the live storytelling night. Who did you invite?

My family. Our adult children, Renae and her husband, Brent, were able to come. Our son, Ryan, and our daughter-in-law, Casie, attended, along with our grandson, Logan. My granddaughter was able to hear the story. She was born two months after her dad, Eric, died. My friend Debbie and her husband came. She's been my Bible study partner since moving here six years ago. So that was really special.

## What was the impact of sharing your story that night?

So many people empathized with what it would be like to lose a child. It's a fear most parents have. They think they would fall apart. But to hear you can get through it and find joy in the process because God can use Eric's story? That was surprising to them. Also, I knew people might cry during the story. Even if you don't have children, you can relate because you had a parent or someone who you loved dearly that you didn't want to let go of yet.

**You've really kept your audience in mind when you share your story. I love how you've embraced both the gift of storytelling and the gift of receiving a story.**

Our church serves a Thanksgiving meal after service, and this year we sat down with two couples who were also retired, maybe a bit older than us. It was a nice group of people to sit and talk to, and we talked about our kids, knowing my story was going to come up one way or another. Eric was also one of our kids, and while we have not had him by our side for 16 years, he's definitely with us in spirit. So, I shared my story, and their mouths were wide open. One of the gals was asking a lot of questions, so I asked: Have you felt this kind of loss? And she had.

She looked at me and immediately started crying. She had lost her nephew. Not her own child, but a nephew. And you could just feel the grief she had. I was just so privileged to be a part of helping her talk about it, not in a threatening way, because I was not going to sympathize with her, but in an empathetic listening way. I didn't offer any suggestions on how to deal with it. I just listened. I have found it is part of God's purpose for me to ask how my story impacts whoever is listening and then find out what I can do to be a better listener.

Some people wanted to take their picture with me after I told them my story. It's meaningful to them. It's really special, but I should not be on anybody's camera. (Laughs.) I try to portray God sent me and not to mind.

**After the class and storytelling night, you were featured on our church's social media in a storytelling series. They invited all the storytellers from the class to share their stories, and yours ran over Easter.**

They did. They took our photos and put my story out there. It took four weeks to share it! People at church are so sweet, and they'd come up after and say: "I saw your article!" Then I'd get tears in my eyes, and I'd ask: "What did you think?" I shared what God's done for me. It's been a privilege and a burden in a way.

In my Bible study, people would come up and talk to me about it. They wanted to give me a hug. Even now, a few years later, people want updates. This last Sunday, a woman wanted to know more, and I shared some pictures of the kids and recapped how the grandchildren are doing.

### You've also spoken a few times, right?

I was invited to speak at another church. I was talking with them about prayer shawls. They had brought one to my dad when he was dying. I told them how amazing it was for him to put it on, to know the whole congregation was praying for him, and to really feel wrapped in God's love. I started sharing about my son, who died in a plane accident. The shawls were an entry point to talking about the plane crash. It was a way for me to witness God's love, how God sent this dream to Eric, how he sent the video, the whole thing. Every opportunity I get, I take advantage of sharing my story. They wanted me to come to a women's group that fall to give a talk.

Then my son's friend asked if I could speak to his church, and they wanted to share clips of the video. I usually just hand out a QR code so people can see the video themselves. We showed three clips. I was scared I was not only going to share my story, but I was also going to reveal my pain because it still hasn't totally left me. I knew I would cry. Usually, I can share my story without any tears, but not with the videos. I told them I'd need a box of Kleenex, and they said that was fine. (You can also view the video at **faithstorytellers.org/resources**.)

Eric's Last Wishes
2006

### How else have you shared your story?

I don't seek out speaking engagements. When God asks, I say yes, but I don't want to go on a speaking tour or anything. There are many other ways to share our faith. The faith storytelling class gave me an "aha moment" that our stories need to be shared. That's our witness, and that's how we help fill in the holes everybody is born with. Some people think it's malts, alcohol, or drugs, but we were made for one reason, and that's for God. It's helped me broaden my storytelling to different things.

For example, my sunglasses. I wear them or hang them on my shirt. They're Lego sunglasses I purchased for Vacation Bible School a few years ago when the theme was "We are built for God." I found them online and just have a ball wearing them, and it never fails. Someone will come up to me and say, "I love your sunglasses," and then I talk about VBS at our church and say: "Did you know you and I are both built for God? It's the only thing that's going to make life worth living." And then I shut up unless someone wants to talk more.

### Do people want to talk after you say that?

Yes, all the time. I was in the checkout line at Walmart, and I met a lady moving to Germany. She's scared because her husband, who is in the service, was being transferred, and he'll be busy and have friends, but she will not know anyone.

It's the first time she's been overseas, and she's got two little ones. I told her, "Though your fear is real, God is really there for you. God will help you through this." And she said, "I've never had any idea of what this God is all about." We must have talked for 10 minutes in the checkout line. That's a God thing because we had a chance to talk.

Another time, we were going out of a store, and a woman was going in, and she held the door for me, and we had this conversation. People were walking by us, and I shared how God fills me up.

Then I hand out my card because I don't want to have that brief encounter and just let it pass.

### What's on your card?

It's a business card with our email and phone number and a website where they can watch our church's livestream service. I used to write it on a piece of paper, but then my husband suggested making cards.

### There are a lot of people who are scared to share their story or their faith. What would you tell them?

It's not something you can just blast out there. I think at a place of work, especially, you have to be careful. If you feel God is urging you, then he's going to find a place and time for you to share. Ask someone out to coffee, hang out afterward, and ask questions in a way that really explores faith with them.

**I knew a public school teacher who had a sign on her desk with a Bible verse. She wasn't allowed to bring it up, but if a student asked questions, she answered. That's what your sunglasses do.**

Exactly. And it's not them initiating. It's the Holy Spirit. The Holy Spirit is the one who creates the crack for the light, and if that light is shining through, they're going to give you that opportunity.

**What advice do you have for people who have a story they want to share?**

First off, pray on it. Get grounded in your own spirituality. Get into your relationship with God and get intimate with God so you and God can talk about what your story is and how God wants you to share it. Take time and really focus on that.

Then write it down because it really helped me be more intentional about what I wanted to share. I'm still open to the Holy Spirit taking me on tangents, but the structure is good. The discipline of editing it and then not using notes to share it was helpful. Even though sharing it onstage from memory still gives me the heebie-jeebies.

**I know! Everyone is scared of that. We had multiple classes, and every single person was able to share their story from memory without missing a beat. I've seen it over and over again. It's scary before you do it but so empowering after.**

Because you get to the point where your story is authentic, and it's coming out because it's your story. It's not something you're faking. At the first class, Mark, my husband, was dumbfounded when he found out he was going to share his story onstage. I don't know if I forgot to tell him or if I didn't say it on purpose. I'm not sure, honestly. (Laughs.) But he's sitting there and looking at me like: What did you get me into?

He didn't come in with a story he wanted to share. He's led a pretty smooth, carefree life, and he didn't want to share my story about Eric, even though it's his story, too. We talked about it, and he decided to share about his stroke. It wasn't until later that he realized he was so close to a completely different life if he hadn't gotten to the hospital on time. He hasn't shared that story in public since. I think he would if he was called on, but he's not going to volunteer it, ever, and that's OK.

**He doesn't volunteer it with people he just met at a church dinner?**

No, never. In fact, he gives me dagger eyes if I even look like I'm going to ask him to share it. (Laughs.) That's OK. I can't be the Holy Spirit for him.

## WAYS TO SHARE YOUR STORY

Pat passed away in November 2023. Our conversation was the last time we spoke. She was an outgoing and optimistic woman, unafraid to ask friends and family to wear tie-dye to her funeral.

"She wanted to worship and praise God for all he has done," her daughter wrote. "She wanted a party with a dance floor (so) people would dance like no one's watching. But the most important thing she wanted us to do is point to Jesus."

I respect how Pat took every opportunity to share her faith. It's how God designed her. But it's not how I'm built. And it may not be how you are, either.

Like Pat, I can engage with strangers, but it took years of working as a journalist to overcome my apprehension. Most introverts I know would never randomly strike up a conversation.

Nor am I wired to debate theology or defend the faith through close study of scripture. When referring to Bible verses, I can never remember the book or chapter. I'm grateful for those who do. I've listened to their podcasts or read their books as I wrestled with Christian teaching. (See books and podcasts I recommend at **faithstoryteller.org/resources**.)

What I can do with confidence is tell my story. I don't need notes to remember how I felt or a textbook to show me what it meant. I can live my faith the best way I know how. And I can share my spirituality — a word, I've noticed, that can prompt nonbelievers to lean in — as it naturally arises in conversation.

How and when these discussions occur always surprises me. Such as the time, a few weeks before leaving the Des Moines newspaper to start my business, a colleague approached and asked if we could chat.

We stepped away from the office to get coffee. Once we settled into a booth in the corner, she began her story. The hospital stay. The doctors warning against her favorite activities. The lifelong condition and its emotional weight.

I asked questions: What happened? What do you mean by that? Can you give me an example? I empathized, acknowledging her pain and turmoil as real. It was something I knew far too well. And I prayed for God to give me the word to say. To speak or not, to share or stay silent.

When she asked about my experience with herniated discs in my neck and back, I responded the best way I knew how: With my personal story. I told her what happened, how I felt, how hard it was, and how I adjusted.

I kept my story in first person. I didn't want to tell her what to do or believe. I just wanted her to know she wasn't alone. My injury also shook my sense of self. It brought me to a place of surrender and the beginning of faith.

I wasn't "evangelizing," a word I've grown to dislike. I was simply sharing both sides of the story, as any journalist would do. My physical and spiritual stories are irrevocably intertwined.

I don't know if our conversations changed her beliefs. Hopefully, I didn't dissuade her. I didn't use bullhorns or guilt-inducing billboards. I didn't give a fire-and-brimstone lecture or engage in what might feel like high-pressure sales. I didn't argue one side of a theological debate or bring up church history or how different verses might apply.

I listened, prayed, and shared my story with the words I felt God brought to mind.

It's the approach God gave Moses, a father of the faith. After seeing the burning bush and hearing God's call to lead Israel out of Egypt, Moses protested the assignment. He lost confidence and doubted that he could do what God was asking of him.

"I have never been eloquent," Moses said in Exodus 4. "I am slow of speech and tongue."

"Who gave human beings their mouths?" God said. "Who made them deaf or mute? Who gives them sight or makes them blind? Is it not I, the Lord?"

"Now go," God continued. "I will help you speak and will teach you what to say."

Like Pat, I don't believe I can "win" someone to faith. That decision is theirs to make. All I can do is point the way.

To go, as God said to Moses, and to trust.

## KEY CONCEPTS AND APPLICATION

- **Pray about how and where to share your story,** and follow where the Holy Spirit is leading. Just as Pat said, God will create the opportunity.

- **Feeling nervous or hesitant about sharing your personal story is normal,** especially if it requires public speaking. Pat wore neon-colored sunglasses, hoping to start a conversation with a stranger, but she still got the "heebie-jeebies" at the thought of sharing her story from a stage.

- **The Holy Spirit opens opportunities for conversations about faith.** Allow his divine intervention to unfold naturally. Pray for guidance on what to share and surrender the outcome — their decision to believe is between God and them, not you.

- **Don't worry about the number of people who read or listen to your story.** Those are metrics businesses use to measure influence, not God. If your story moves one person, then it makes a difference. You might not know the details until you get to heaven.

CHAPTER 8

# FACING FEARS OR DOUBTS

"There's a wildfire."

My editor walked to my desk at the edge of the newsroom, which was quiet except for the buzz of the police scanner. The televisions near the front were tuned to local and national news, what we deemed "Mission Control," as it mimicked NASA's iconic approach to monitoring information during launches up the road at Kennedy Space Center.

I was covering a Saturday breaking news shift. There were three of us on duty: an editor, a photographer, and me. I'd barely sat down when my editor told me to go.

The rest of the day's team was scattered. The sports reporters were at games or on their way. The copy editors and designers, responsible for proofing and laying out the next day's edition, were brewing their first cup of coffee. The printers would be in later to run the presses. And the delivery drivers would arrive for the last leg of the journey in the early morning hours.

My name would byline the story, but I wasn't alone. There was a team behind me: newsroom colleagues with different skills and responsibilities and the unsung heroes of printing and distribution.

"I need you to go," my editor said, and I wrote down the address, masking my anxiety as agitation. Competitors would be at the scene, and as the local daily paper, I knew it was my responsibility to "own" the story.

This direct match up, which pitted my reporting against others', unleashed my insecurities. While other reporters loved the adrenaline rush of breaking news, I dreaded it. Instead of rising to the challenge, I worried I'd buckle under it.

I was telling myself a story I was too ashamed to admit to anyone else. I falsely believed I wasn't smart or skilled enough to be there. That my editors made a mistake when recruiting me across the country. That I wasn't cut out for the high-intensity news we covered on this stretch of Florida.

I threw a few reporter's notebooks into my purse, checked to ensure I had pens and water — who knew how long I'd be out there — and parked as close as I could. Sirens blared behind me. A fire engine passed, heading in the direction I was supposed to go.

I walked down the block and checked my phone's map against the smoke rising in the distance. Then I spotted Craig, a veteran photographer who'd chat with me in spare moments about his mother, a retired educator, and her take on stories I wrote.

Not all photojournalists enjoy working alongside writers, but Craig and a few others seemed to enjoy the collaboration.

"Oh, thank God," I said when I reached him. "Have you heard anything?"

"I'm just walking," he responded, his eyes focused on the plume of smoke rising above the trees. "I'm just walking, and I'm going to see what I find."

"I'll walk with you," I said.

He nodded.

It was a silent agreement built on mutual respect, past assignments, and previous conversations. We'd work the story as a team. God's answer to a prayer that never crossed my lips.

He photographed the firefighters. I interviewed them. We'd spot homeowners and I approached them. I'd introduce myself before he held up his camera, a soft opening that put people at ease.

I'd learned to notice body language: whose hands were on their hips and whose arms were crossed. Who caught my eye as I approached, who shifted their stance, and who looked away.

I knew it would be hit or miss, as it always was in this line of work, so I listened carefully to their response. If they didn't want to talk, we respected that. If they spoke in short, stilted sentences, I recognized their indecision. In so many words, they were telling me they had nothing to say.

There were always people who wanted to talk. I just needed to find them. Sometimes, it was the person directly affected; other times, a relative or neighbor. Occasionally, someone seemed relieved or even thankful we were there to tell their story.

Another journalist put this in perspective for me. I wasn't just a reporter, she told me. I was representing the community. Through my presence and my desire to share their story, they were reminded that they mattered. And their community cared.

My fear dissipated. Somewhere between connecting with Craig and talking with homeowners, it slipped away. Gone but not defeated, I knew from experience. It would lurk in the shadows until the next opportunity to rear its ugly head.

## DON'T LET FEAR STOP YOUR STORY

More than a decade later, the same fears that surfaced as a reporter were acting up. Doubts and insecurities rattled my resolve to step into the unknown by publishing this book.

"What's wrong?" my husband asked during dinner one night.

I couldn't form the words. Instead, I sobbed into my plate of pasta, overwhelmed by the week's cascading events: The "quick" errand that grew into two hours stuck in traffic. The multiple times I hurried home, dropping everything to take shelter in our basement in central Iowa before severe weather arrived. A book deadline that could no longer be pushed back.

**Even the most prolific writers experience fear.** It's a familiar mix of dread and excitement. It can show up as writer's block or procrastination. Nearly every storyteller I worked with faced moments of doubt or apprehension. Just as you may be now.

It's common to worry about falling short of your standards or other people's expectations. Or to question if you're a "real writer" or whether you have the courage to speak onstage. "I could never do that," I heard audience members whisper at live storytelling events. "Not in a million years."

I added this chapter because too many people told me they loved reading the faith stories you'll find in Part II. They found the process of crafting a faith story intriguing. They wanted more stories and hoped others would submit theirs for consideration in future Faith Storytellers books. Yet they told me: "I'd never do that."

It was heartbreaking to hear. Most storytellers I've coached are excited yet apprehensive at the start. Their anticipation grows as they progress, something they must persevere and pray through, an expected and natural part of the faith storytelling process. Even Moses, who God called to lead Israel out of Egypt, initially resisted!

Once they did, however, sharing their story was so invigorating that **many faith storytellers found other ways to speak about their beliefs and experiences.** They spoke at TEDx talks or churches or ministry events. They wrote self-published and traditionally published books. They were interviewed or shared their story in Christian magazines, on podcasts, and with secular media. Like Pat, who lost her son in a plane crash, many followed the Holy Spirit and shared their story one-on-one.

What is stopping so many of us from sharing our stories? One of my friends believes it's the devil, a fallen angel that spins up lies and makes us fear the next step. He stands in the doorway and makes the necessary leap of faith look terrifying. The fear he stirs up tempts us to retreat, and unfortunately, many do.

I didn't used to think the devil was real, not beyond what I learned as a kid in church, anyway. As I grew older, blaming the devil seemed like a convenient excuse. A way to shirk responsibility or accountability.

I also can't deny the darkness. I've seen the headlines from across the ocean and down the street. There's no escaping the pain and destruction. The wildfires and tornados and hurricanes. The evils of murder and terror and abuse. It would be foolish to deny it.

**Yes, the darkness exists, but it doesn't have to trick us into losing hope.** If you keep looking at your shadow, as someone once explained to me, you never turn around to see the source of light.

The good news is we don't take this step of faith into the unknown alone or through our own might, discipline, or will, as some modern gurus falsely preach.

"For when I am weak, then I am strong," Paul writes in his letter, an often-cited verse from 2 Corinthians. A contradiction if you believe you must beat fear. Or it's the truth if you believe as I do: There is a spiritual battle, yes, but that's not the end of the story. It continues.

Through the cross, Jesus beat the devil. Our side already won.

## THREE THINGS STORYTELLERS NEED TO PERSEVERE

I admitted my fears about finishing this book to a friend as we walked near downtown Des Moines. After listening to my long list of concerns, she challenged me.

"Have you prayed?" she asked when we stopped to fill up our water bottles.

I turned to look at her, letting the words sink in.

"I didn't think of that," I said, kicking myself. "Why didn't I take my own advice?"

When we tested the Faith Storytellers Framework at my church, we prayed at the start and end of each session. Through prayer, we humbled ourselves. We recognized God's strength and presence, and we invited him into a deeper relationship as we allowed ourselves to let go of our worries and rely on him.

**I believe three things are needed for storytellers to confidently walk through the challenges of sharing their stories with the world. Prayer, community, and preparation.**

As a journalist, my fear dissipated when I partnered with colleagues and focused on the story, not my apprehension. In the storytelling class at my church, students shared their angst and empathized with each other. Today, I rely on my husband, friends who are always up for a long walk, and a small group of women who meet each week to study the Bible and encourage each other.

I also know the importance of doing what we can. As a reporter, it means asking questions that get to the heart of the issue and accurately reflecting it in the newspaper. As a ghostwriter, it means multiple conversations to focus the story, revisions to structure it, and edits to refine and polish it. As a speaker, it means practicing your story out loud and preparing for the event.

Before each faith storytelling night we held at my church, we practiced the evening's sequence. Storytellers sat in the "on deck" chair, which meant they were next, and they walked onstage in the order they would appear. They adjusted the microphone stand to their height. Or they took the mic off its holder and moved the stand behind them and out of their way.

They practiced starting their story by saying it out loud. They heard how the mic amplified their voice, which took one storyteller by surprise, and she gasped in astonishment. In the safety of an empty room and surrounded by friends, we laughed. A deep belly laugh prompted one storyteller to lean against a chair and the one onstage to blink away tears.

They tested how far the microphone could move before it picked up the speakers' feedback. They practiced ending their story: They paused, said "thank you," and exited the stage.

I walked them through the common pitfalls of a live storytelling show. They agreed not to stop to point out a mistake they made midway through. Not to stop and back up their story to share something they forgot.

"Just keep going," I told them. "The audience will never know."

If they tripped or made a gaffe, I told them not to worry about it. To make a joke of it. It didn't have to be funny. They just needed to acknowledge it happened and show they could laugh at their own mistake.

"The audience will be holding their breath," I said. "They're waiting to see how you react. That's the tension you'll feel in the room. But as soon as you invite the audience to laugh with you, they'll join you. They'll relax, and so will you."

I taught them everything I know about faith storytelling. The same knowledge I shared with you in this book.

The storytellers did their part, too. They took each step of the Faith Storytellers Framework one at a time. They shared their story first with a partner and then with a small group in class. They told each other what they liked and what resonated the most. Words I hoped they'd remember and reflect on before the event.

They practiced by memorizing their story by saying it out loud. Those who treated their story like a script were likely to forget onstage. But those who repeated it out loud committed it to muscle memory. They didn't need notes because it wasn't a performance. It was their story, which they knew better than anyone else. Even if the words were different, they knew what to say.

The only thing to do now, before friends and family and community members arrived, was to pray. It's the last thing I'll invite you to do — just as my friend invited me — before you release your story into the world.

## PRAYER PROMPT:

God, I'm nervous about sharing my story. I'm worried about what people will think or say. I'm doubting myself and whether I can do this. I'm tempted to quit or to stop before I begin. I also know I've made it this far for a reason. I've felt your nudge to craft and share my story. I want to follow through.

I can't do this alone. I need your help. And I need your people. Help me find the people who can walk with me on this journey, who can support me just as I will support them.

Lord, help me focus on your light. The ray of goodness you're shining down on me, the light surrounding me and holding me up. The radiance of the faith story — your story — I'm about to share.

Help me let go of my story. Help me trust you with it. Take my story to the next leg of its journey. Pick it up and finish what I cannot: Help my story find and connect with the people you always intended it to reach.

## SEEKING GOD'S STORY AFTER THE STORM

Fear is a tool. An emotion to heed when there's a real threat. It heightens your senses and makes you aware. Here in Iowa, I've learned to notice when the sky turns a hazy green or when birds grow quiet outside. To listen for the sirens that warn of a potential tornado or deadly storm.

Fear can also be confusing. I've already explained the overreaction it can cause. Insecurities can spin into a spiritual tornado, ripping our confidence and courage away. As storytellers, we can take the snide comments to heart instead of letting them pass. Or we can stop ourselves before we begin.

The opposite can also occur. After the fifth or sixth time sirens went off this month, it was tempting to ignore them. To look out the window instead of going downstairs or venturing outside to see what's developing in the sky.

**As storytellers, overconfidence can prompt us to take unnecessary risks.** We can push too hard to tell our story or for others to listen. We can disregard helpful feedback or ignore the Faith Story Guardrails, which are designed to keep our story in check and ourselves and others safe.

The third time I sheltered in my basement this week, the forecast came true. A tornado cut through a small town an hour away. Wind gusts were up to 185 mph. Wind turbines crumpled like empty cans underfoot.

I watched on television as the weatherman explained what was happening on radar. A tornado was on the ground. In less than a minute, it cut a diagonal line through the town of Greenfield. We later learned it damaged or destroyed more than 150 homes.

A short while later, the weatherman told us to stay home. The storm was almost past, and he'd worked in our community long enough to know what to expect next. He addressed it directly.

Stay put, he told us. Wait for people to ask for help. They need time to process the shock.

That night, I looked through pictures of the tornado's path with my husband. We were devastated. Houses missing roofs and siding. Basements or concrete slabs where homes once stood. Semi-trucks tipped over, pieces of cars in trees, wood planks and siding strewn on the ground like autumn leaves.

Years before, I watched a similar scene on the national news. A well-known anchor covered a similar level of destruction after a tornado tore through a state farther south. He showed the destruction, explained what happened, and invited a country music star who lived nearby to join him on-screen.

The anchor sympathized. Then he asked what he claimed everyone at home was thinking: Why would anyone live here?

I was stunned by the question. Then angry.

Why would he ask that?

Did he ask victims of California wildfires why they lived in the woods? Or, while covering a hurricane, why people live along the Florida coast?

The singer answered flawlessly. The people, he responded. The community.

He shifted his stance and looked around. Have you heard the stories of neighbors helping neighbors, he asked, or the strangers going above and beyond?

These stories are just starting to emerge from Greenfield, a town where historic buildings line the city park and town square. Neighbors pulled a man out from under a pile of debris. He couldn't believe he was still alive. A woman's house collapsed around her, yet she emerged with only bruises. Others made a makeshift stretcher to get the injured to medical care.

"God saved me twice," one woman told a local television reporter. "He saved my soul and now he's saved my life."

No one is allowed into town right now. Only residents who can prove their address, the responders searching the wreckage, and the journalists assigned to cover the story. They'll write the first draft of history as they document what happened and share it with anyone who wants to read or watch or hear or see.

I wish the tornado never happened. That homeowners never had to rebuild, or families never had to bury loved ones. I don't know why these things happen. All I know is that they do and that I need to remember the words of a priest, a message that comforted me after a church burned down: Focus on what comes next.

Look toward the horizon. If we believe what Jesus told the disciples in John 16:33, darkness is to be expected, but it's not the end of the story. "In this world you will have trouble," Jesus said. "But take heart! I have overcome the world."

Officials keep telling us to stay home. Don't travel to Greenfield to help. The time will come. Soon. Just not yet.

The desire to help is so strong where I live that the first instinct my neighbors have is to go. To support the town however they can, in whatever way they need. It's heartwarming to see.

I can't help but shake my head at my memory of the national news anchor.

Why wouldn't you want to live here?

Who wouldn't want to live in a community that must be told to stay home? To not help?

Journalists are continuing to report on the tornado's aftermath, as they should. Hopefully, they also serve as a reminder, as I once did. That the people of Greenfield matter. And that their community cares.

They're also sharing the stories I always look for after disasters. Stories I believe reflect God's love and constant presence. The close calls and near misses. The moments of gratitude and relief and community strength.

I invite you to look for these stories, too. To seek out the hope that appears after the storm passes and the once-hidden sun comes into view. To see these as the faith stories that they are: reminders of his love and presence and saving grace.

## KEY CONCEPTS AND APPLICATION

- **Fear and insecurity are real and may be spurred by the devil to stop you from sharing your story.** As Christians, however, we believe Jesus defeated him on the cross and won the war.

- **Sharing your fears or doubts with a trusted friend or with others in your community can help alleviate your concerns,** as can praying for God's strength, protection, and guidance.

- **Weigh the teachings of spiritual leaders against Christian teachings.** Some may seem to speak the truth and even accurately describe the battle against darkness, but if their solution doesn't align with the Bible, be wary.

- **Practice your story out loud without a script.** It's OK to use different phrases or words each time, so long as you can share it without stopping or backing up. Once you've committed it to memory, share it with a trusted friend and then a small group of three or more. Ask what part of your story resonated, which will help you see the impact your story may have once shared.

- **Do what you can to understand the environment,** which can reduce anxiety about the unknown. Ask to see the room you'll be speaking in. If possible, practice walking onstage, adjusting the microphone, or starting or ending your story.

- **Darkness exists in the world, but God does, too.** When confronted with disaster or destruction, look for ways God's goodness shines through. Seek out the near misses and close calls. Look for how people are helping and supporting each other.

# PART II:
# 40 STORIES OF FAITH

*"He did not say anything to them without using a parable."*
*(New International Version)*

*"He always used stories to teach them." (International*
*Children's Bible)*

*— Mark 4:34*

# THE HOLY SPIRIT, A PLANE CRASH, AND A VIDEO THAT CHANGED MY LIFE

## BY PAT JACOBS

My husband Mark and I have been married 47 years. We have three sons and one daughter, four children by marriage, and 18 grandchildren. We are just an ordinary family, bound together by the love of Jesus, living to point everyone we meet to his love.

In 2006, on a cold and rainy November afternoon, our daughter and I packed up four grandsons, ages 7 and under, into our van to meet their dad in Williamsburg, Iowa, about halfway between our home and where they lived.

We were excited to have the boys with us for the weekend. Their parents, our oldest son Eric, and his pregnant wife Heather, had been busy cleaning and getting ready for their fifth child.

While I packed the boys in Eric's car, he told me the weekend had gone well. But at church that morning, he had felt the Sneaky Spirit — what we sometimes call the Holy Spirit — suggest he invite people from church to sign up to help Heather in case of an emergency. So, he did.

He asked people to help pick up the older boys from school, come over and play with the other kids, and be with Heather in case she needed a ride to the doctor's office. To call my husband and me in case of an emergency, as well as his coworkers. He also asked someone to be in charge of the whole list, to call all these people, just in case.

He hung the list on the refrigerator and was so glad he could go out of town the next day and not have to worry about Heather and the boys.

I told him that was a pretty good idea, but he assured me he could take no credit. In our family, we know these little nudges come from the Holy Spirit. And we know to act on them.

## A DEVASTATING TURN OF EVENTS

The next day, Monday, Nov. 13, Eric had a work meeting in LaPorte, Indiana. He planned to fly commercial instead of with his coworkers, who were flying on a private airplane. Eric just didn't feel good about it.

At 11:30 that Monday night, we got a phone call from his coworker saying he didn't want to worry us, but Eric hadn't come home yet. Heather had been having contractions, but there were people with her at the hospital and at the house with our grandchildren. Before saying goodbye, he said it was very possible Eric might be driving a rental car home.

Then he said the private plane his coworkers had boarded for Iowa had crashed right after taking off. They were not sure if Eric was aboard.

Mark and I both thought it was very possible Eric could be driving home, so we turned on the porch light, and we sat down and prayed, prayed, and prayed some more. Our phone rang a few hours later. It was 3:30 a.m. We got a call from the coroner's office in Indiana confirming Eric's backpack and wallet had been found at the plane wreckage site.

We knew then that Eric had died. It was a strange feeling. Our 31-year-old son was not going to experience his daughter's birth or watch his children grow up. Or know his youngest would be a daughter.

We knew the next thing we had to do was to pack up our bags and head to see Heather and our grandchildren.

## FINDING A MESSAGE FROM ERIC ABOUT GOD

The outpouring of love from their church family over the next few days was amazing. So was what happened next. In preparation for a meeting with the insurance agent, Heather went down to gather documents from their safe. When she did, she found a DVD marked "Eric's last words."

We learned that, four months earlier, Eric had a very real dream that he had died early. He felt he needed to record his thoughts because he felt they were from the Holy Spirit. Maybe he was paranoid, or maybe this was proof God truly does work through people's lives.

"Hello everybody," he said as the video started. "If you're watching this, something bad has probably happened to me." He assured us he did not plan on dying right away, joking that after he was old, he would throw the video out without ever showing it to anybody.

But there we were, watching it. Watching him. For 38 minutes, Eric told us many things. He told his brothers they had to move back to be role models for his boys. He told his sister she needed to read the Bible six times through and be the spiritual mentor for his children. He told Mark and me that we needed to move to Ankeny and be there for the kids, which we eventually did. At the end of the video, Eric had us all say the Lord's prayer together, and it was such a blessing.

In the midst of my sadness, I was so proud of him for witnessing to us in this way. He told us to show the video to anyone we meet who doubts there is a God. "Because I am proof that there is a God. God talked to me, I acted, and this is my proof."

At his celebration of life, we were surrounded by hundreds of townspeople, friends, and family members. It was truly a celebration. In the midst of our sadness, we felt supported and loved, which we know can only come from God.

I noticed one couple in particular. The wife, through tearful eyes, said, "I hate to say this, but if it hadn't been for Eric's death, we probably would be getting a divorce." They told me they had been talking and decided to stay together.

The first thing that came to my mind was Psalm 118:24: "This is the day that the Lord has made, let us rejoice and be glad in it." In the midst of my sadness, I could see joy. And I could share it with others and be happy for them. It was a blessing from God, and I knew Eric would be right alongside me and say, "Good job, Mom, encourage them! That Sneaky Spirit is at it again!"

The one thing I have experienced over and over again these last 12 years since Eric died is that God is always with me, guiding me. It has not been easy. There have been many extremely difficult times. Through it all, my faith has grown dramatically. I have learned to lean into sad and hard times, just like Mary and the disciples did. And I know there is one thing I will never doubt. God is alive and real. My son lives because my Redeemer lives.

# HOW A POST-IT NOTE REMINDS ME OF GOD'S PRESENCE

## BY TRACY SOUZA

A navy-blue Post-it Note is taped inside the back cover of my Bible. In silver gel ink and beautifully scripted penmanship, it reads: "Mrs. Souza, we love you!" It was signed by my fourth-hour girls' Bible study, complete with an exclamation point and a heart doodle.

I've carried this message of encouragement around for more than two decades. It was written in 2000 by one of my ninth-grade students at Oklahoma Bible Academy, where I taught for a short time while passing through Enid, Oklahoma, courtesy of the U.S. Air Force.

I carry it as a reminder that God is ever-present in my life, even when I'm not paying attention. That encouragement can come from unlikely people in everyday places and often when I least expect it. It's particularly reassuring on the days that feel extra difficult.

The day my students stuck the Post-it Note to the top of a stack of ungraded catechism assignments was extra hard. My heart hurt deeply from grief. I was in my late 20s and barely a second-year teacher. My maternal grandmother had passed away the day before.

I was trying to keep my head up and work through to 3 p.m. I fought back tears, just waiting for the bell to ring so I could lock my classroom door and let the grief slip out in the form of an ugly cry. I hadn't told my students about my loss, but they could sense something was off. And so appeared the small, personalized sticky note, which was slipped quietly onto my desk. It said:

"Mrs. Souza, we love you!"

## IN JOY AND PAIN, GOD WAS THERE

Now, more than 20 years later, the note still brings tears to my eyes. A reminder God sees my hurt and heartache, and he reaches into my life to lovingly pour out his extraordinary mercy and grace. It has been a source of strength and encouragement many times over the past two decades.

It was there through the fear of the days immediately following the Sept. 11, 2001, attacks when my then-husband was deployed, and it was there when the exhaustion of being a mama to little ones threatened to overwhelm me. Most recently, it soothed my heart when my marriage of almost 24 years ended in divorce.

A heart doodle in silver-gel ink: "Mrs. Souza, we love you!"

As I pile up trips around the sun, every once in a while, I stop to take in the panoramic sight in the rearview mirror, and I can see God in the details of every snapshot. He was there when a car accident could have taken my life or the life of my unborn daughter. He was there in the split second when my son could have drowned in the deep end; instead, I heard his small voice cry out above the noise of the crowd. And he was there in the unlikely friendships, the laughter of my teenagers, and the magnificence of a sunrise in the Grand Canyon.

It's amazing to me — as I survey my 35-plus years of walking with God — the number of times he has whispered to me: "I see you. I know you."

Some days, my life brims with simple joys, such as when my coffee is a perfect shade of tan. Other days, it's overflowing with grief and heartache and brokenness, leaving my soul raw and exposed. But regardless of where my day falls, on the mountaintop or in the valley, I know I'm not on this journey alone.

## BEING A REMINDER FOR OTHERS

Now, it's my turn to be someone else's Post-it Note.

Sometimes I leave my kids a note on their bathroom mirror telling them they are seen and loved. Other times it's taking a meal or a gift to the new parents next door. I smile at a stranger as we pass on the sidewalk or tell the lady standing in line at the grocery store just how lovely she is.

So I carry my Post-it Note to remind me I am not the only one that needs to be seen.

It reminds me to be present where I am and to encourage others walking alongside me in this messy, overflowing life.

I carry it as proof of how God uses the ordinary to accomplish his extraordinary.

Every detail in life carries with it a message whispered softly to the very core of my longing soul: I am seen. I am known. I am loved.

# WHAT I LEARNED ABOUT GOD WHILE SERVING IN THE ARMY

## BY RUSSELL E. GEHRLEIN

In the spring of 1978, I sensed a clear call to professional ministry. I was leaning toward Christian education or youth ministry. I knew I wanted to do something with my life that would have eternal value.

After graduating from college, I interned in junior high youth ministry for two years. My wife graduated in 1982, and we moved to Portland, Oregon, for me to start seminary. The following spring, I found a position as a church youth director.

I enjoyed it immensely — until it came abruptly to an end in the summer of 1985. My youth ministry position was terminated when the church decided to hire a full-time Christian education director.

I worked a couple of odd jobs after that, but none provided for my wife and infant daughter. I decided to drop out of seminary in December 1985 to take care of my young family. After much prayer, soul-searching, seeking counsel from family and friends, and weighing the pros and cons, I felt God leading me to enlist in the U.S. Army in February 1986.

It really was an answer to prayer, and yet I felt guilty.

I knew God led me to join the Army, but I felt it was a humbling step backward.

I had done all I could to pursue my dream of becoming a youth minister, but God had closed that door. I had to find a "secular" job, and I falsely believed I was a second-class Christian.

I never lost faith in God; I knew he was with me. But I felt a combination of disappointment in myself, doubt in my ability to sense God's direction, and anxiety about what the future would hold.

## A BREAKTHROUGH

Much of what I had heard in my late teens and early 20s from teachers and speakers at campus ministry events affected my thinking about secular work in a negative way.

With a heavy emphasis on evangelism and discipleship, I was exposed to a view that the earth was going to burn when Jesus returned. Going into vocational ministries such as missions or church work was strongly encouraged over "worldly" careers.

The doubt it created followed me into my Army career. During my first assignment at Fort Stewart, Georgia, I did not believe my work as a soldier had any direct impact on the kingdom of God. It was frustrating not to use my spiritual gifts on a full-time basis as I would if I was a minister.

In March 1988, I was sent to Korea for a one-year tour while my wife, three-year-old daughter, and two-month-old son stayed back with family. As the year went on, I found myself becoming confident in my role as a sergeant. I saw glimpses of God's blessing in my work. For example, I competed for and was selected as the noncommissioned officer of the quarter for all of Korea.

In my last few months there, I read the book "Your Work Matters to God," by Doug Sherman and William Hendricks. They tore apart the myth of "sacred" vs. "secular" work and explained the intrinsic and instrumental value of everyday work. One particular quote grabbed my heart and opened my eyes.

"(I)n addition to salvation — obviously a need with eternal implications — mankind has many other needs," they wrote. "Just because many of them are temporal needs does not diminish their importance to God, nor does it diminish the value of the work done to meet those needs."

What I understood for the first time was God could use me — a U.S. Army nuclear, biological, and chemical specialist — to meet the needs of my fellow soldiers whom he loved enough to die for. I found I could use my technical expertise to maintain protective masks and train soldiers on how to properly wear and use their equipment, which would better prepare them to survive on a battlefield.

I realized I wasn't wasting my time. In fact, I was doing the Lord's work. I began to have peace about my decision to join the military. The decision to reenlist was easy, and I committed to serving six more years.

## MY UNDERSTANDING DEEPENED

Wherever I was stationed, I met Christians who did not see how God could use them as a soldier. I knew God was guiding me and wanted others to see it as clearly as I did. He was using my spiritual gifts of teaching and encouraging others.

I began teaching Sunday school classes and Bible studies with other military families. I studied verses and the theology of work. I became grateful for the opportunity to serve the Lord every day, knowing my work has eternal value.

I served on active duty for 20 years before retiring as a master sergeant in October 2006. I currently work for the Department of the Army as a civilian employee at the school where we train soldiers in my same specialty. I go to work every day knowing God is with me and is working in me and through me.

I believe God is a worker — which means all work has value — and he has called us to work with him. To expand and care for his creation. And I believe God is present with us, whatever the title or position may be.

# GOD WAS WITH MY FAMILY AFTER A FARM ACCIDENT TOOK MY DADDY

## BY MARY GRACE JOHNSON

I loved growing up on a small farm not far from Bridgeport, Nebraska. And I loved watching my daddy work around the farmyard, taking him lunch in the corn or wheat fields, and seeing his love for tinkering with old cars.

I had four siblings, a dog, several cats, and other animals to play with and enjoy around the farmyard. I was also blessed to have Christian parents and a loving family around me, including all my cousins and both sets of grandparents.

When I was eight years old, on a hot and sunny day in May 1971, my mom gathered the five of us siblings, and we piled into the pickup to take lunch to the field where my daddy was working. It was past lunchtime, we had all eaten, but he hadn't come home.

Unfortunately, the pickup had a flat tire, so my mom worked on changing the tire while we kids waited nearby. It wasn't quick work, and I could tell she was uneasy with the task. My sister thought she seemed nervous and agitated as we waited. After a while, she finished, so we all crawled back in and started out of the driveway.

We didn't get far. Mom stopped the pickup when she spotted two cars behind us on the road, which she recognized as our grandparents' cars. They approached the pickup, and they told Mom that my father had been killed in a farm accident while he was disking a field.

Cries and sobbing took over. My mom cried out. Then she nearly passed out. I wasn't sure what happened, but I was struck by fear. I felt a heavy weight in my chest. My sister started running to the house, only to be called back by our grandparents.

When they explained to us Daddy was gone, the tears came. Our grandparents surrounded us, providing comfort in what was the worst moment of our young lives.

We drove back into the yard and went into the house. Things seemed to move very fast as we packed up some things to take with us to our extended families' homes. My grandparents made plans for each of us to stay with different family members because there wasn't a place where we could all stay together.

At one point, my sister dropped onto the bed and prayed, "Dear God, please take Daddy to heaven." At that moment, I realized God would answer because Daddy had a personal relationship with God. He spent his life taking us to church, teaching us to pray, and sharing about God through his words and actions. He knew the Lord.

While I knew Daddy was in heaven, I was still afraid — afraid to see Mom's pain and afraid for the future.

## GRIEF DOESN'T STOP, AND NEITHER DOES GOD

Life changed. I grew up and went to college out of state. I met the love of my life and married. We lived on the farm where he grew up. During the next six years, we had two children, a boy and a girl.

While our children didn't get the chance to know Daddy, they shared a close bond with my mom. I found comfort in knowing I learned a great deal from him while he was on this earth. I shared stories of Daddy's love and playful nature with my children and grandchildren.

My grief didn't stop there, however. I lost my precious grandparents. In 2009, my eldest sister passed away from ovarian cancer. Her death was a huge blow, and the depression and anxiety that followed were a lot to handle.

After a time, I felt I had learned to live with grief. But then, in 2019, it all came rushing back. My daughter and her husband lost their sister-in-law in a car accident. At 40, she left behind a husband and six children.

During the visitation and funeral, my husband and I stayed with the two youngest, ages 4 and 7, as they played outside in the driveway. At times, the older boy would say, "My mommy died," or "I won't see her again."

I assured them they would see their mother again in heaven, and they felt comfort in knowing that. During lunch after the funeral, the youngest sat on my lap. Memories of Daddy flooded back, and we shared a moment of comfort.

## UNDERSTANDING GOD IN A DEEPER WAY

After the funeral, God took hold of my heart with a new purpose. I could help others who faced the loss of a parent or close relative at a young age.

It hasn't been easy. I am still learning so much about trusting God, and it is a daily experience of putting everything into his hands and following his purpose for my life. But I have joy in my heart knowing my daddy and other loved ones are in heaven with Jesus.

While I continue to struggle with anxiety and depression, I have learned to lean on my Heavenly Father, the Comforter and Deliverer. And the Holy Spirit, who helps me put things into perspective.

And I'm getting there with God's saving grace. You see, God sent his Son to die for me so I might have eternal life if I choose to accept it, though I am so undeserving. I have shortcomings. Flaws. Lack of trust. Fear.

Yet God continues to provide forgiveness throughout my journey so I may be reunited with him one day — just like he did for my daddy.

# MY CREATOR: A STORY OF GOD'S DAUGHTER

## BY HEATHER L. EBERHART

I was born with a port wine hemangioma birthmark on my face. That's a lot of big words to say half my face is red and half isn't. The birthmark surrounds my left eye entirely and continues in my mouth and down my throat.

At first, this was a major concern for the doctors and my parents. Doctors believed I wouldn't live past the age of seven, and if I did, I would suffer from social delays and learning disabilities. Because of the nature of this type of birthmark, and its location on my head, the doctors believed pressure could be building around my brain.

They advised immediate treatment, which would also lighten the pigmentation and reduce the risk of vision loss. Within the first few years of my life, I had nine laser treatments.

Thankfully, the doctors said my brain was functioning normally. Any further treatments would be cosmetic. With the advice of my doctors, my parents stopped treatments. They hoped my birthmark would lighten on its own over time.

Once red, my birthmark had lightened to a shade of pink. You could still notice the birthmark. I was physically healthy, but elementary school was hard. Middle school was excruciating.

From my earliest memories, I knew I was different by the way others treated me. I endured years of standing in the Shop 'n Save checkout line in Zelienople, Pennsylvania, with my mom and hearing people say to her: "Oh, is your daughter OK? It looks like she got punched in the face!"

I was always confused when a stranger commented, but I rarely had time to react. As a young child, my mom was there. She would step in and protect her baby girl.

But relying on momma bear can't last forever. I was called "two-face" in middle school, and I was frustrated. I falsely believed God made a mistake when he made me.

Within a week, I was in the doctor's office, wanting more surgeries to make me look "normal." I was tired of the comments, tired of feeling different, tired of always having to explain my face to others. I was confused and embarrassed and I wanted to feel normal.

My mom sat with me in the doctor's office, holding my hand. In order to start the procedure, I needed local anesthesia. When the doctor came at my eye socket with the largest needle I'd ever seen, I panicked. I cried, screamed, and told the doctor, "No!"

I looked to my mom, desperate for help, and she said, "Heather, I will support you either way, but you know I think you are perfect the way you are. Just like Grandma Lee used to say."

## STOPPING THE TREATMENTS

On the day I was born, my great-grandmother told my mother to mark the backs of my baby pictures so no one would get them confused with my brother's photos. It seemed unnecessary when one of your children had completely normal facial features, and the other had half her face covered in a reddish-purple birthmark.

Grandma Lee saw us differently. She saw two beautiful babies. Period.

Grandma Lee spoke truth to my family in 1987. She told us we could not judge a person by what he or she looks like, because they are valued, loved, and adored by our Father in heaven. She repeated this belief throughout the first 12 years of my life. And she didn't stop until the day she went to be with the Lord.

I don't remember her words exactly, but they rang true for me and for my parents.

After that day in middle school, I stopped seeking medical treatment. I knew it was the right decision. Just like Grandma Lee, I believed every cell in my body — including the ones making half my face red — had been made in his image.

## HIS PERFECT IMAGE

I can stand in awe of God's amazing work. He created the sky, the land, and the seas. And I can smile knowing he made zero mistakes when piecing me together.

Today, I believe covering my birthmark or trying to hide it is like saying to God, "I know you are perfect and all, but you really screwed this one thing up."

It reminds me of Ephesians 2:10: "For we are God's masterpiece. He has created us anew in Christ Jesus, so we can do the good things he planned for us long ago."

Today, I am a confident, healthy, 32-year-old child of God, and I thank my Creator daily for making me the way I am.

# FOLLOWING GOD'S PROMPTING TO SALT LAKE CITY

## BY COURTNEY GRACE WATSON

"What if the circumstances we fear the most are the ones that will afford us the most abundance?"

I came across this question while reading on a flight in February, and I immediately wrote it as a note in my phone. I didn't know why, but it seemed important.

I looked at the note occasionally over the next five months. Every time I read those words, they seemed important. Some days I came across them and stopped in my tracks. On other days I sought them out and questioned what it was that drew me to them.

During this time, I was considering joining a church mission team going to Salt Lake City to share the Gospel. I hesitated, however. Fear crept in any time I considered saying yes to this trip — it was out of my comfort zone. I had only done service-oriented mission work before, never a mission specifically for evangelism.

And yet, I was curious and felt the Spirit nudging me to go despite my fears. So I did.

Then the world seemed to fall apart as the COVID-19 pandemic closed businesses and moved travel plans. Suddenly, the trip seemed out of reach.

## THE POWER OF PRAYER

Despite challenges and the spike in coronavirus numbers, I believed God was asking me to take the risk of travel. I can't explain it other than

I felt a pull toward Salt Lake City. I couldn't shake the thought that I needed to get on that plane and make the trip. So I did.

The first night in Salt Lake, I joined others on the mission team to hike to a spot overlooking the area. When we reached the top of the trail, we prayed for the city and its people as we watched the sunset over the mountains. I began to feel something shift. I knew I was in the right place.

The days that followed were spent largely in prayer rather than evangelism due to COVID-19. We spent time at the homes of church members who had been unable to attend services in person, praying with them in their front yards, talking with them, and enjoying each other's company — socially distanced and with face masks, of course.

We also spent time at places where we could pray for groups of people. We prayed over teachers and parents in the parking lot of schools. We prayed over local, state, and national government officials in front of the state capitol building. We prayed over store workers and business owners at their workplaces. We prayed over areas of town the Lord had been faithful to work in and areas of town we hope to see him work in the future.

The shift I felt on the first night became a piece of my heart, which was breaking a little more with each "Amen."

Honestly, I haven't seen how the Lord will take these prayers and bind them together, but I do know this: A trip I feared had created abundance.

I saw how praying for members of the body of Christ and our greater communities is a powerful spiritual practice. It deepened my trust in his faithfulness. That God will change the hearts and lives of those lifted in prayer as well as those doing the lifting.

It reminded me of John 10:10, which says: "I came that they may have life and have it abundantly."

## ABUNDANT LIFE

I've often defined abundance as a number in a bank account, a title printed on a desk, or a house full of people and possessions. But Jesus didn't come into the world to give me my dream job or health or money or status. He came to offer life. He came to offer eternal life in the kingdom of heaven.

Looking back, I can see how the question — "What if the circumstances we fear the most are the ones that will afford us the most abundance?" — came to mind anytime I was trying to decide whether to travel to Salt Lake City. I just didn't make the connection until now.

Through the trip and the fear that surrounded it, I found myself back at the foot of the cross, immensely grateful for a savior who came to earth to offer a life more abundant than anything I could find here.

I realized the depth of the Lord's graciousness toward me, a grace that has absolutely nothing to do with my own capacity. I saw the depth of my pride: How I took for granted growing up surrounded by churches proclaiming the Word of God, being raised in a family who loved the Lord, and having the privilege of sharing the Gospel.

Above all, I recognized the faces of people who have not yet learned of such grace. The Lord was undoing my heart. He was shattering the perceptions of my own pride and worthiness of the Gospel, and he was binding up a heart and a life lived on mission.

# A NEWSPAPERMAN INVITED THE COMMUNITY TO HIS DAUGHTER'S BAPTISM

## BY TIM WALTERS

During my sophomore year of high school, I received literature from various colleges around the country. To me, it didn't matter. I had a plan: To attend the University of Florida, get my journalism degree, then come home to work for the newspaper I grew up reading, Florida Today.

Everyone told me University of Florida was incredibly hard to get into and I should expand my options. But I had faith my good grades and test scores would be enough. As a teenager, I let my decisions be guided by faith because I believed God would lead me where I needed to go.

I only applied to one college, and I was accepted.

In the Fall of 1995, I moved to Gainesville to attend UF. I majored in journalism and earned my degree in May 2000. At the time, Florida Today generally didn't hire journalists out of college. They liked to see some experience on the resume. So I took a job at a small newspaper in central Florida and began work just five days after graduating college. After working two other newspaper jobs, Florida Today came calling. Again, my faith paid off.

Through the years, I've done some amazing work, including coverage of sports, space, news, features, and so much more. I expanded my skill set by learning how to shoot and edit photos and videos.

My favorite accomplishment occurred in 2014, when my daughter, Isabella, was born. And, of course, I wrote about her in the newspaper.

## SHARING MY FAITH IN THE NEWSPAPER

A co-worker suggested I use my sense of humor to write a parenting column where I told funny stories while also showing dads can be just as capable of parenting as moms. In May 2014, "Daddy Duty" was born.

I used it as a way to discuss not only my parenting but how faith drove how I parented. I aimed to be the best dad I could be and to set an example for others to follow. I wanted to show people faith comes with morals, and with morals comes the ability to do the right thing.

One time, I wrote a column about Isabella's baptism and invited the community to attend. To my surprise, the Mass was packed, including dozens of non-parishioner readers who accepted my invitation.

Many told me they weren't Catholic but wanted to see my daughter baptized. They seemed thankful I had extended an open invitation to the public.

Soon after, a young Catholic club asked me to speak at their monthly meeting because they thought I was brave to publicize my religion and my daughter in the newspaper. I told them I don't see it as a problem. Quite frankly, I don't care if people don't like that I discuss my religion in the open. My life is mine, and I won't be ashamed of it. I'm comfortable with who I am.

I also wrote honestly and vulnerably when doctors found a tumor on Isabella's spine when she was only 2 years old. I shared photos online and kept readers updated on her condition.

The initial diagnosis left me shocked more than scared, but as soon as I wrapped my head around it, I went into confidence mode. The tumor was found by accident when doctors looked for a different ailment. That told me God wanted it to be found. Our medical crew was incredibly experienced and competent. I continued to tell my wife, my mother, and my in-laws everything would be OK.

Inside I was shaken, but my belief God would take care of Isabella gave me a calm I still don't fully understand.

Through this tough time and her surgery, readers were so kind in sending emails, handwritten cards, and leaving voicemails. I knew people enjoyed my column, but as I walked Isabella through the medical procedures, I realized my readers were like an extended family.

Many of them prayed for our family, and in the end, our prayers were answered. The surgery was a success, and Isabella hasn't had any residual effects.

I decided to end the column in June 2019, right after Isabella's graduation from preschool. I notified readers three months in advance to let them know when the final column would run. I felt it was time for her to have her privacy and start the next phase in her journey.

This was really tough because people had come to see Isabella as an extension of their family. She was recognized almost everywhere we went. She was "the baby from the paper!" It felt like she was Brevard County's granddaughter.

## PASSING MY FAITH TO MY DAUGHTER

In 2019, Isabella began kindergarten at a Catholic school. I wanted her to have the same Catholic bedrock and education I received.

I look forward to taking her to church every Sunday. Watching our 5-year-old do the sign of the cross and hearing her say the "Our Father" makes my world brighter. At Mass, she brings joy to those around us. She picks where we sit, and she's found a favorite spot next to an older lady who comes to church alone. Isabella will say good morning and shake her hand during the welcome. It's wonderful to watch how much Miss Sully really enjoys sitting next to our little one.

Having Catholic roots means Isabella not only has a family who loves her but will always have the gift of religion to fall back on. Her faith can keep her strong in moments of weakness.

I've now been at Florida Today for more than 17 years. The hard work and ethics instilled in me as a youngster helped me survive and overcome a continually shrinking industry.

It's also helped me be a good father and husband. But the best gift? The blessing I didn't expect?

Sharing God's love with my daughter.

# A 'TINY' CHRISTIAN COLLEGE REBELLION

## BY KEELA DEE VAUGHN

I was born and raised in the church, and I always thought church would be part of my life. I accepted Jesus into my heart when I was eight. I was a leader in my youth group, and I was never out past midnight, except when our high school band attended an out-of-town football game.

I grew up in Lubbock, a West Texas college town. I had a strong support system of family and friends, and I knew all the best places to eat. I was comfortable. But the year I graduated high school, a lot of things changed.

With Texas Tech University right there, I decided to stay close to home for college. But my parents decided to move five hours away to be closer to my two older siblings. Then my high school flame of two years broke up with me.

I was devastated. For the first time, I felt truly alone in my hometown.

During the first semester of my freshman year, I hardly left my dorm room. I was under a cloud of depression and dealing with all the post-breakup stages of grief: Hoping he would come back, burning all his photos and letters, trying to stay "just friends," and crying myself to sleep.

### A 'TINY' CHRISTIAN REBELLION

Once I entered into the acceptance phase with my ex, I tried looking for other things to satisfy me.

The church I grew up in didn't have a college group, so I eventually stopped going. I figured it was about time for me to have a rebellious phase. Just a "tiny" Christian rebellion to check off my college bucket list.

I went dancing and drinking and dating. I put God on the shelf. I attended church a handful of times during college, and I got suckered into a Christian retreat. When I did allow God to speak to me, I heard sermons on Luke 15.

The first time, I rolled my eyes and barely paid attention. The second time, I waved it off as a coincidence. The fifth time? I started wondering if God was trying to tell me something through the story of the prodigal son.

The more I heard about the Gospel story — how the father met his son on the road after he was estranged for years — the more I realized God wanted me to come back to him. But I was ashamed. I didn't want God to see who I had become. I didn't want to face my decision to reject him for worldly pleasures.

I was afraid God would be mad or disappointed with me. I falsely believed I had to clean up my act before I could run back into his arms.

## CELEBRATING A DAUGHTER'S RETURN HOME

It wasn't until I started a relationship with my now-husband that I decided to better myself. Colton and I had been friends since high school, and he had a similar story: growing up a "good kid" and then, during college, putting faith to the side.

We dated on and off because we each had some maturing to do. During the final semester of my undergrad, we decided if we got together again, we were not going to break up.

We falsely believed we needed to get "right with God." I stopped dating around, we stopped going to parties, and we started reading the Bible. We also found a church home together.

I finally felt the arms of God wrap around me, just like the father did with his son in Luke 15. But as I grew closer to my Heavenly Father, it suddenly hit me: I did not need to clean up my act in order to run back to him.

In the parable, the prodigal son did not realize his sinful ways, repent, and then run back home a clean, valued member of society. He came back because he was hungry. He still smelled like pigs. But once he neared home, his father ran to him and wrapped him in a hug. They celebrated with a fattened calf.

That's what I have to keep in mind, no matter where I am in my walk: God wants me just as I am. He will open his arms and greet me with love, even as I continue to struggle with sin.

God never needed me to "get right" with him; in fact, I'll never be "right" with him. I'll always need his redemption. But I can run toward him, mess and all, and receive his warm embrace.

# HOW I'M USING MY VOICE TO BRING LIGHT TO OTHERS

## BY AMANDA CHIRELLI

My faith took root in 1984, the day I was born with a lifelong disability: Cerebral Palsy.

Because of the diagnosis, which limits my movement, I have always needed help with everyday tasks most people take for granted, such as bathing, dressing, meal preparation, and toileting.

I couldn't run, jump, or play like my able-bodied siblings at our home in Ocean County, New Jersey. If I went to see a friend, I had to worry about whether their house was wheelchair accessible.

My family worked hard to make sure I had the same treatment and opportunities as everyone else. I attended and graduated from a public school and was active in school activities, such as choir. But most importantly, my parents instilled in me an unshakable faith in the Lord Jesus Christ and the knowledge I could conquer any obstacle life throws at me.

### SEARCHING FOR DIRECTION

A big turning point came after I graduated from high school. For the first time, I felt I had no direction. I didn't know what programs were available for people with disabilities, and there weren't a lot of transportation options.

I've always tried to stay upbeat, but I couldn't shake the sadness and loneliness. I thought there was no purpose for me in life. It was a dark time, but I knew as long as I kept my faith and kept on praying, things would get better. And they did.

About five years later, in May 2007, I enrolled in a work program for people with disabilities. I was able to improve and enhance my work skills. About a year later, I was offered a part-time job as a branch greeter for Investors Bank. At 24, I finally earned my own paycheck, made friends, and worked in the community. I finally felt I had a purpose and a place in the world.

The job was an answer to my prayers. But little did I know God also had other blessings in mind. About two years after starting my job, I was asked to speak publicly and share my story at a benefit dinner for a nonprofit agency that helps people with disabilities. Sharing my story with others gave me a sense of purpose.

When the COVID-19 pandemic hit in 2020, the bank's branches closed to the public. After 12 years with the company, I was no longer able to work. I was reminded of the time following high school when I felt darkness. I didn't know what was next. I prayed for God to shine a light and show me what direction to go.

## LIVING OUT MY PURPOSE

The day after I prayed for guidance, a friend asked me to join her church group for people with disabilities called Wonderfully Made. Through this faith community, I learned to better listen to and talk to God. I've since become a leader of the group, as well as a member of the church's welcome team.

At the same time, I was accepted into an advocacy program through Rutgers University called NJ Partners and Policy Making. I'm learning to become a better advocate for myself as well as other people with disabilities. When I graduate from the program, I will sit on advocacy boards and be a voice for people with disabilities like myself. I'll be telling my story to more people.

I've started sharing my story with others. I was recently a guest on Jill Dobrowansky's podcast called "Feed Your Spirit." I spoke about living with a disability. I told her about my first time getting into the ocean as an adult, thanks to a beach chair a relative made for me. I spoke about how God has shaped my destiny. It was freeing.

Through the many twists and turns in my life, I've learned as long as I keep my faith and love in Jesus Christ, there are no limits to where he can take me.

Whenever I need encouragement, I think of Proverbs 3:5-6: "Trust in the Lord with all your heart, and lean not on your own understanding; in all your ways acknowledge him, and he shall direct your paths."

When darkness comes, God is my light.

# YOU ARE MY BELOVED

## BY DIANE HASKINS

My story begins once upon a time, but not so very long ago. I was at a very low point in my life. I was struggling with deep sadness and despair. My heart was wounded from years of trying to measure up to who I thought I was supposed to be as a wife and mother. I felt like a mess, inside and out. I questioned my self-worth and wondered how God could love someone like me.

One night, I remember going to bed in tears — struggling with my identity, worth, and value — and begging God for an answer to my deepest question, "What do you really think of me?"

His answer was clear and unmistakable. It was the beginning of my rescue and a journey to discover my "inner beauty," my true self in Christ.

He said to me, "You are my beloved."

The truth of this settled in quickly, and I fell asleep with a peace I hadn't experienced for a long time.

## GOD'S RESCUE PLAN

What happened over the next several years was the beginning of God's rescue plan. He started by transforming my thinking. He renewed my mind and changed my narratives to begin to see him, myself, and others through his eyes.

He used a lot of different things — time in his Word, amazing Christian authors and speakers, and something called the Apprentice Series at my church in Iowa. Through the study, I discovered I could trust in a good and beautiful God who saw the real me and loved me just the same.

My false narrative of "you'll never be enough" was replaced with truth. "I am one in whom Christ dwells and delights, and I live in the strong and unshakable kingdom of God."

He was restoring my joy, giving me hope. There were moments when I struggled with feelings of "not good enough." There still are. But I also know God's rescue plan isn't finished.

## A DOG NAMED BONNIE

It was Father's Day 2011, and my husband and I were hanging out, spending the day with our daughter at a local mall. Our daughter had to work, so we said our goodbyes. I imagined we would just head home for the day, but God had other plans.

My husband suggested we go to Petco. When we walked in, we saw an adoption event. I noticed all the animals were in kennels except for one little dog sitting on a blanket in the middle of the floor. She was wearing a bright yellow vest with the words "Little Miss Sunshine" in red letters on the back.

I walked over. She was so nervous she was shaking. As I bent down to pet her, I realized she was completely hairless.

She looked up at me with her sad, big, brown eyes, and I was completely in love. Her name was Bonnie. She was a puppy mill rescue dog. Her foster mom gave me permission to take her picture, and I didn't hesitate.

We walked out of the store, but I couldn't get her out of my mind. The following day, I printed off her picture and put it up at work. I looked at it multiple times a day.

As you can imagine, it didn't take long before I officially adopted Bonnie and brought her home, and our stories started to intertwine.

## A BEAUTIFUL MESS

You see, Bonnie is a mess — inside and out. Her ears are bent and wrinkled from frostbite and infection, she has issues with her skin, and she lost all her teeth.

She suffers from anxiety as a result of her time in the puppy mill and spins around in little circles that I imagine are the size of the cage she lived in. In many ways, we are alike. Some days I feel a lot like the way she looks.

Bonnie's "beautiful mess" became a mirror for my own life. Just as she learned to trust me, I'm learning to trust my Heavenly Father. In times when anxiety causes her to spin, my presence can calm her.

In the same way, when I am filled with anxious thoughts, and I question my worth and identity, I am learning to rest in God's truth. His presence quiets and calms my mind and my soul.

I see more to Bonnie than what's on the outside. And my love for her is a reminder of how God sees me, inside and out, just as I am. And God loves me just the same!

My identity in God is secure. I can live from that place, trusting in God's good and beautiful rescue plan for my life. As it says in Matthew 10:30-31: "You, beloved, are worth so much more ... God knows everything about you, even the number of hairs on your head. So do not fear."

# THE PAIN OF LOSING MY MOTHER LED ME TO MY PURPOSE

## BY SONYA JOY MACK

My mom was my safe place, and I was her joy. Sonya Joy to be exact. She gifted me my name because I was meant to "spread joy to the world."

By the age of five, her friends called me her "mini-me." With the same permed, fire-red hair and short, fluffy build, it was easy to see why.

As a child, I would crawl on my mom's lap — a trend I continued when my age and size made it unusual — and lean my ear to her chest to listen to her heartbeat.

I would stare out the window of our home in the small town of Algona, Iowa, watching the corn roll in waves for miles and the birds perched in the nearby elm. I'd imagine our future together, my mom by my side when my children were born, and traveling together once we both had more than our modest lifestyle could afford.

### TRYING TO NUMB THE PAIN

In 2005, my first year of school to become a physician assistant was rolling to an end. Our dreams for the future were within reach. But then my mom was diagnosed with ALS, a progressive neurodegenerative disease that slowly breaks down muscles. Its victims are unable to walk, talk, and eventually, breathe.

Five years later, my family gathered around a hospital bed in the living room of my childhood home, medical equipment crowding the once ample space. I put my ear to her chest to listen to her heartbeat. Only this time, it was for the last time.

We buried my mom in the depths of winter, our feet crunching the underlying snow as we walked to her headstone. I was 29 years old. And I was so afraid.

I didn't know how to live without her. I feared I might forget the honey smell of her Avon perfume, the tinkling sound of her laughter, or the way her eyes crinkled at the sides when she smiled.

God and I have always been close, a faith-by-heart mentality born more from a "feeling" than anything learned from a book. A trait I inherited from my mother.

I knew God was there, even when I couldn't explain or rationalize it. But in my pain, and without my mom as my compass, I wandered spiritually.

I couldn't understand how God — who was supposed to be my loving Father — would allow me to suffer pain so crippling. Much less consider it part of his greater plan.

Lost and alone, I tried to numb the pain by doing what I do best. I picked up a pen and wrote. I'd always found God there before, scrawled in words that flowed from my hand. I was desperate to find him once again, hoping he could soothe my despair.

As I wrote, words rose as if they were mine, but they weren't. They originated from my core, far deeper than my humanness. They came from the one who created me: "You're meant for something bigger, something different."

For years he repeated these words, tattooing them in indelible ink on my heart. No matter my confusion or frustration, they never altered.

"You're meant for something bigger, something different."

Not understanding what the words meant, I threw myself into hobbies and passions, thinking one would be my "something bigger and different." I tried voice and acting lessons, but nothing felt right. Trying desperately to restore my relationship with God, I continue to put pen to paper, scrawling out my pain.

## A CALLING: YOUR PAIN HAS PURPOSE

It was a calm summer night, nearly seven years after my mom's death. I was 36 years old, listening to the crickets chirp outside my bedroom window. My daughters, now 3 and 5, slept in their nearby rooms. I cried out in desperation to God.

"What does this all mean? I just want this pain to go away. I just want to find my joy," I screamed, "Where are you?"

His voice came to me as clearly as if it were my own.

"You find your joy when you find me. Through me, your pain has purpose."

Shaken but more alive than I'd been in years, I flipped frantically through my journals, the place I knew I had found God before. There — in bold, capitalized letters — were words such as faith, hope, love, choice, and inspiration. Spiritual principles meant to lead me down the right road.

I had suffered so much heartache, including traumatic births, the near death of a child, and chronic physical pain. But that night, I realized my pain was the road to "something bigger, something different."

The words in my journal weren't just words. They were a framework for living, feeling, and growing from the pain in my life. These principles were the roadmap to living a life of joy. A message God fashioned me to share.

My pain, connected with the promises of God, was a message to every woman who was hurting from the deepest places. There is more than just hope on the other side of pain. There is purpose.

I came to realize God's true intentions, and my relationship with God is closer than ever. He didn't create my pain, but he allowed me to go through it so I could grow through it.

When I gave my pain to God, it became so much more than the hurt in my heart; it became a pathway that led to my God-given purpose.

# LEAP OF FAITH: FOLLOWING GOD'S CALLING TO COLORADO

## BY NICOLE PILGRIM

In 2012, our family of four traveled to Colorado for summer vacation. After a week of soaking in the panoramic views of the Rocky Mountains and wearing light jackets during unseasonably cool August evenings, we declared it to be the most beautiful place we had ever seen.

We headed back south to Texas, and somewhere between multiple pit stops and hundreds of miles of highway, my husband and I casually agreed. One day Colorado would be our future.

We both grew up in the piney woods of East Texas. We met in high school, attended Texas A&M together, and settled in the bustling Dallas-Fort Worth area to raise our family.

Our children attended our neighborhood school, where I worked as a first-grade teacher. I felt blessed to teach alongside some of the best educators I'd ever known and also some of my dearest friends.

Life wasn't perfect, of course, but it was humming along smoothly. My 11-year-old daughter was thriving in piano lessons and musicals, while our nine-year-old was excelling in gymnastics. They had a close-knit group of friends and loved their school.

I enjoyed living life alongside our best friends, frequently getting together for playdates and dinner dates. Our family was only a short drive away. And I loved leading a Sunday school class with my husband at church.

We were approaching our late 30s and content to grow old in the home we loved. So it came as a complete shock when — smack in the middle of our comfortable fairytale life — I heard God telling me it was time to let it all go.

## HEARING GOD'S CALLING TOGETHER

Three years had passed since that vacation in the mountains, and I hadn't thought about it since. We always assumed it would serve as our quaint little retirement spot down the road. And yet I felt restless. A holy unrest I couldn't ignore.

When I prayed about the source of the discontentment, God continued to gently whisper it was time to make a move. He was calling us to Colorado.

I was filled with awe that God graciously made his will crystal clear. I was also amazed to discover crippling fear and delirious excitement could coexist in my heart.

Several weeks later, while my husband and I were on a walk, I confessed I felt God calling our family to move. After a few moments, my husband stopped walking, looked at me, and told me he felt God telling him exactly the same thing.

We walked in silence. Neither of us had ever felt such clear and specific guidance from God before. Yet I wrestled with doubt. My emotions ping-ponged between the excitement of a new adventure and the pain of an inevitable goodbye to friends and family.

We agreed to continue praying about it. The implications of such a decision weighed heavy on us both. We prayed that if this was God's will, he would open doors and create opportunities.

God responded with a resounding yes. He did not take away the desire to move. Instead, it only intensified. And my husband was given the opportunity to stay with his company while working remotely.

As God's will became more clear, my heart grew more divided. I felt enormous guilt for plucking our kids from their idyllic childhood. The future I planned for them disappeared like a balloon set free, drifting away before my eyes.

As a mother, I feared how deeply this would affect them. I was terrified of leaving the comfortable life we knew. But I could no longer ignore God's calling. We were finally putting into practice the very faith we claimed to have.

## DISCOVERING GOD'S FAITHFULNESS

I diligently researched top school districts. Once we explored the Fort Collins area, we knew it was a perfect fit. Less than 12 months after our conversation, and four years after our Rocky Mountains vacation, my husband and I loaded up a U-Haul and drove 15 hours north to our new home.

The initial excitement soon dissolved into homesickness. The first several months felt like an uphill battle. Our daughters, in fifth and seventh grades, struggled being the new kids at school.

After a hard day, I could no longer meet my best friend for coffee at a moment's notice. My husband missed the close relationships he'd made through church and his softball team. My heart broke when my girls couldn't call a close friend to come over and play.

We continued to pray through the rough patches. We prayed that God would remind us of his promises to never leave or forsake us.

As the months ticked by, things became easier. My husband had never been happier in his role at work, and working remotely from home — long before the COVID pandemic of 2020 — suited him perfectly.

Our children soon formed close friendships and found joy in choir, cross country, volleyball, and youth group. We found a church home and built new relationships with members of our small group Bible study.

We grew closer as a family and made incredible friendships. And we continue to have meaningful, extended visits with our family and close friends back in Texas.

Five years have passed since we took a leap of faith and moved to Colorado. For every provision we prayed for, God provided in abundance. And just as he promised, God was my anchor in a storm of uncertainty.

Stepping out in faith built a foundation of trust and dependence on God that changed our lives. God has yet to reveal his specific purpose for calling us here. Even though we don't know his ultimate plan, I am so grateful we said yes.

I'm reminded of Peter's story in Matthew 14. When Jesus called Peter out of the boat, he had doubts. Yet the Lord was calling him to obey in the midst of his fear. Every time I read this story, I am reminded of how God richly blessed Peter's life by weaving his obedience into one of the greatest miracles in the Bible.

It isn't always easy for me to obey God, especially when I can't see the outcome. But I've learned obedience leads to blessings. And I can trust that releasing my life into his hands creates a life far greater than any I could create on my own.

# HOW GOD HEALED MY HEART AND CHRONIC PAIN

## BY MEGHAN DEWALT

I was diagnosed at age 11 with bilateral hip dysplasia. I was walking with an increasingly heavy limp, often with a cane, and using a wheelchair to go to a local amusement park. I was living life — a hard but good life with chronic pain.

Missing everyday outings such as ultimate Frisbee, hikes, or bike rides chafed and hurt my heart. On other days I soldiered on, took ibuprofen, got coffee with friends, and tried on fancy dresses in Macy's. By the time the fun times were done, I was gritting my teeth and sighing — sad and angry beneath the surface.

For a shy girl in those tender, awkward, formative years, the looks, pitying words, and questions shaped me.

I had learned in Sunday school the refrain, "God is good all the time, and all the time God is good." Yet what was happening to me was not good. It was miserable.

I knew God was theoretically good to all who call on him. Good in the sense he couldn't not be good. But I also heard what was left unsaid, and I falsely believed God didn't want any questions asked.

### QUESTIONING GOD'S GOODNESS

On my 22nd birthday, I had a major hip surgery. It should have partially relieved my chronic pain. But it was undone by an infection two weeks later, setting my recovery back six weeks. It turned my whole life upside down.

Deep in the throes of bed rest, waiting on a hip replacement after an infection, I struggled with questions about God:

If God is good, why did he let me have malformed hips?

If God is good, why didn't he let the first surgery work?

If God is good, why hasn't he given me a husband and family, which I want more than anything in this world?

Confronting these questions shut me down. I was unwilling to face the fact that I, a good church-going Christian girl, did not trust God for much more than my eternity. That I did not trust and believe the whole truth of the Gospel — that it was for both my past sins, present struggles, and future sins.

Four surgeries and 11 months later, my life changed. I was back up on two good feet. Getting a new job, making new friends, trying online dating — I had a life to live. And I desperately wanted to find a husband.

Free from the confines of measuring my energy and weighing my decisions against my chronic pain, I took living pain-free for granted. I had brief moments of gratitude: "Huh, I'm walking through a bookstore at my leisure and in no pain. Thank you, God!" But more often than not, my emotions were tangled and suppressed in the deep recesses of my heart.

It wasn't until a really tough holiday season six months after my last surgery that my heart began to turn. God was calling me back, and I responded. Beneath my loneliness and longing for a husband was a deeper longing for church. I never felt I had fit in at the churches I grew up in, but this time, I wanted to find a true church home.

## GOD IS GOOD, AND HE IS GOOD TO ME

I wasn't sure what I wanted in a church. A denomination different than what I knew appealed if only for its uniqueness. But going somewhere completely by myself was intimidating. And also freeing.

I Googled and read church websites until I happened upon one in a cute little borough 20 minutes away. I promised myself I'd go at least three or four times, and not just "church shop" at someplace different every week.

I never left. There, on the red plush pews of an early 1900s Presbyterian church — now a community church — my heart healed. I began to experience and then know deep in my bones that God was good, and God was good to me.

God was good not because he'd healed my hips, not because he gave me a church home and months later guided me to my now husband and a Haiti missions trip.

No — God was good because he became real to me.

I encountered God on Sundays in church, then during my daily Bible reading, and then in small group Bible studies with people who exhibited the welcome and love of God.

Despite having prayed the sinner's prayer at age five, it took four surgeries as an adult for me to surrender my whole heart to him. God was so tender and good. He picked up all of my pieces and put them back together into a beautiful whole.

# RESULTS THAT CHANGED MY LIFE

## BY MARYBETH EILER

I sat in the doctor's office, awaiting the results of my latest MRI. Fifteen months prior, a rare, aggressive tumor was surgically removed from my left calf. Three months earlier, scans revealed concerning evidence of potential regrowth.

Emerging side effects and symptoms began to take on new meaning as I watched and waited to see what the next set of scans would reveal. Would they confirm the tumor's return or provide the evidence I desperately wanted — it was mere scar tissue?

The MRI results came back with conclusive evidence. The tumor was back and more aggressive than before. With surgery no longer a viable treatment option, my doctor referred me to an oncologist to recommend alternative options.

As a rare disease with no standard FDA-approved treatment, I had limited options to halt the tumor. We were up against the clock as the tumor's rapid growth began to impair the mobility of my leg as well as creep dangerously close to a nerve.

If treatment options were exhausted, amputation would be the remaining alternative.

My new reality slowly began to set in. The path forward was not clear-cut — it was full of unknowns and little control. Questions began to surface:

"God, why is this happening to me?"

"Aren't I too young to be dealing with something like this?"

"What about all those plans I had carefully laid out?"

My life as a carefree 25-year-old was gone. Weekly hikes and yoga classes, regular trips outside of Indianapolis, and the honeymoon phase of a new marriage came to a halt as my husband and I discovered the true meaning behind "in sickness and in health."

I was contending with a new normal — one that encompassed far more doctor appointments, far less focus at work, and far more uncertainty about what the future would hold.

As the weeks progressed and the need to find an effective treatment plan grew more critical with each passing day, fear and worry began to tighten their grip.

"Would we find an effective treatment plan?"

"Where was God in the midst of this pain?"

"Surely he had not abandoned me," I thought.

## MOMENTS OF GRATITUDE

As we began to try different treatment options, I continued to seek answers. I stumbled upon the book "1,000 Gifts" by Ann Voskamp, which highlighted an important truth: Giving thanks in all circumstances is what we are called to do as believers.

Was it possible to give thanks in the circumstances that surrounded me? I had my doubts but felt led to give it a try. I began filling a gratitude journal with whatever I could find to be grateful for in the midst of the messy circumstances surrounding my life.

Day after day, I opened up my journal and wrote whatever came to mind: The ability to cook dinner on my own for the first time in months, new books from the library to enjoy while recovering from chemo, no longer needing a medication that helps with pain management.

A full night's sleep in a comfortable bed. A walk around the neighborhood with only the aid of one crutch.

In the beginning, it often felt forced. Some days it was a real slog to find a few things to be grateful for, but over time, it became easier to find the good. As I noticed the good, even during hard days, I began to see how God was present with me in the midst of difficult circumstances.

I began to see God at work in my pain and suffering. When life felt completely out of control, he was still there, ever-present in both big and small ways. A card in my mailbox on a day I needed extra words of encouragement. The provision of a friend who suffers from chronic illness. She could relate to my fears and provide the encouragement I needed.

The more I focused on the good in my life, the more gratitude I found. Paying attention to the good allowed me a glimpse into the ways God was at work in my life. I was amazed as I began to notice God weaving together little details — details I would not have noticed if I hadn't had my eyes open to see.

## THE WHISPER OF A CELEBRATION TO COME

One day — almost two years into chemo treatments — I had a nagging feeling. I was getting MRI results, and although I had no reason to believe there would be a change in my course of treatment, I whipped up cupcakes to share with my team of caregivers.

The day began like any standard chemo-infusion day: labs followed by an appointment with my oncologist.

Except this time, my sister could come with me. She hadn't been able to attend a round of chemo in more than 10 months, partly due to having a baby and partly because appointments had moved to Tuesdays when she worked. A few months prior, she had requested this Tuesday off to have an extended weekend.

Then my dad surprised me by showing up in the waiting room — catching me completely off guard. He said he had a hunch and just needed to be there.

Feeling a little unsettled by the looming test results, I handed out cupcakes to the check-in staff and nurses, then waited for my appointment to begin.

During my oncology appointment, my oncologist shared the unexpected news. I was done with treatment.

Instead of heading to the chemo infusion center, I delivered the remaining cupcakes to nurses who had walked the journey with me. I shared the good news, and we cried tears of joy as I rang the bell to signify the end of my treatment.

The day had unfolded in a way only God could have planned. The whisper of a celebration. Freeing my sister's schedule. Prompting my dad to visit. When the good news came, I was surrounded by my husband, father, and sister, cupcakes in hand.

Those little details? I'm certain I would have missed them if I hadn't been looking for God's fingerprints and writing them in my journal.

God is not some distant God who only sweeps in to perform big miracles. He is a constant presence. I simply had to open my eyes and my journal to see it.

# TRUSTING GOD'S PLAN WITH MY SON

## BY AMY EILERS

Ever since I was a little girl, I've wanted to be a mom. In kindergarten, I would come home from school and spend hours in our backyard taking care of my dolls and making mud pies in my kitchen made of bricks on our cement patio.

I would dress up my cat Tippy in doll clothes and push him on the swings in our backyard. I would then take my dolls and Tippy for walks in a little stroller, and I would cuddle them and sing to them and take care of them. I am sure Tippy really loved that. Poor cat!

I couldn't wait to be a mom someday. Five-year-old me also liked to be in control. I had my room organized and my clothes and my things just so, and I was frustrated with my sister, whose room I used to call "the pigpen." As I grew older, this need to be in control only got stronger.

To this day, I have a favorite backpack for work. I love all of the pockets and zippered sections allow me to organize my planner, pens, work items, and keys. Each has its own spot.

I grew up, went to college, married a wonderful guy named Mike, and started my career. We traveled, enjoyed time with our family and friends, and finally decided it was time for a family.

I was so excited to learn I was pregnant, and we were blessed to have two beautiful boys during the next three years. And then the real fun began. Mike began to travel more for work and was gone several days a month. My career was also busy and filled with travel, and we began to juggle raising our two boys.

As our younger son entered ninth grade, we began to notice a shift in his moods and behavior. This creative, sweet, funny kid became increasingly sad, overwhelmed, and needy. He began to avoid activities he enjoyed, had trouble getting out of bed in the morning, and began missing more and more school. Everything started to derail.

## MENTAL HEALTH CHALLENGES

What happens when there is a disconnect between my vision of being a mom and the reality of a child who struggles? What was I supposed to do when my child couldn't function in the way he had in the past? For a person who likes to be in control, it started to feel very scary.

After many months of struggle and confusion, our son was diagnosed with anxiety and depression, and I started a many-year journey into loss of control and darkness. I rode the roller coaster of mood swings with my son and began to realize how much my emotions were tied to his. In his darkest moments, I was in the pit of despair with him. And I had a difficult time rebounding.

I couldn't sleep, couldn't eat, and tried to maintain the facade that everything was OK. At the same time, the side of me that likes control kicked into high gear. There were ups and downs, but no matter how much I worked, schemed, and struggled to fix everything and make it all better, I could not change the situation.

It was a place of fear and frustration, and I felt completely out of control and helpless. During this time, I had support from wonderful friends and family, but I couldn't get out of this dark place alone. I felt like I had a huge rock of worry and sadness sitting on my chest that I didn't know how to dislodge.

One of my biggest support systems then and now was my girlfriends at our church's Tuesday night Bible study. One night about two years ago, one of these women shared her story about attending a session of our church's Inner Healing Prayer. Her testimony was powerful.

The ministry is a guided conversation with God led by members of our church's prayer team. It helps you receive healing from spiritual and emotional wounds. I felt a very powerful sense of urgency that this was something I needed to do, and I signed up for a session.

The night of my first Inner Healing, I didn't know what to expect. During the session, I went through the most loving experience of guided prayer with three members of the prayer team. As we prayed, I wept. And I felt a sense of release.

However, when I arrived home later that night and faced the same situation of darkness and chaos, I went right back to that place of helplessness and hopelessness. I didn't think I could be healed until my son was healed, and I was losing myself along the way.

## SURRENDERING

Several weeks went by, and I felt an overwhelming urge to sign up for Inner Healing a second time. As we were going through the process of guided prayer, I was in such a sad, hopeless place. One of the prayer team members suggested I picture my son in my arms and see what God revealed to me.

I pictured my 6-foot, 200 lb. child in my arms, his arms and legs dangled across my lap. I lifted my head and said to God, "I can't do this anymore. I am not in control, and I don't know what else to do but to give him to you."

The most amazing thing happened. I realized I had done all I could do, and now it was time to cease striving and surrender to God. As I was holding my son in my arms, I saw God reaching down and gently taking him from me. I experienced the most overwhelming sense of peace. I surrendered to God and let go. I let God have him.

Once I gave up all my anxieties, fears, confusion, and hopelessness to God, I was in a place of absolute and utter peace. I realized the most loving thing I could do for my son and for me was to give him to God and let his love heal us both.

At that moment, God became real to me. And we began a relationship of faith and trust that changed how I look at the world and, more importantly, changed me.

My son has been on a journey of his own and has come so far with his anxiety. He still struggles at times, but whenever I get down or scared, I know I can reach up and give my son back to God.

God is always there to take my son into his arms. Just like in Jeremiah 29:11: "'I know the plans I have for you,' declares the Lord, 'plans to prosper you and not harm you, plans to give you a future and a hope.'"

God offered me hope. I just had to be willing to surrender and trust in him. And that is a beautiful, hope-filled, and joyous place to be!

# GRIEVING MY MOM AND ALLOWING GOD TO BE THE STRONG ONE

## BY JANA FRALEY

As a young girl, I would sometimes grumble and complain with my brothers about all of the hard work and constant "family time" we endured as Wyoming ranch kids living in the high plains and ranges of the Uinta Mountains.

We lived 10 miles from the small town of Mountain View, and at the time, all I wanted was to live in town so I could ride my bike to my best friend's house.

But ranching is a way of life. We spent each day working together, playing together, and eating three meals a day around the dinner table. We spent long days in the saddle trailing cattle. Feeling fresh air and sunshine on my face. Hearing the sounds of creaking leather and bawling calves. And the constant smell of horse and saddle.

As I grew older, I wanted to be just like my mom. I adored and admired her. She was the epitome of who I wanted to be as a ranch wife and mom.

My mom barely reached 5'2" and was tough as nails. But she also had a gentle, patient way with livestock. When I was 10, I'd watch her work tirelessly to save newborn calves born in the bitter cold. She never showed frustration, just determination, as she coaxed life back into these babies.

More than anything, I wanted to emulate her wisdom and faith. She had boots-to-the-ground faith, which she lived each day.

Shortly before I turned 24, I married a ranch boy from across the state. Mike and I met at the Wyoming State Fair as teenagers. Eventually, we raised cattle and kids at the base of the Big Horn Mountains in Northern Wyoming with his dad and stepmom.

After selling the ranch I was raised on, my parents bought a ranch just a few hours away from our place. We would get together to help with big jobs like branding in the spring and shipping calves in the fall.

In June of 2015, when I was 44 years old, our whole family, including my brothers and their families, gathered at my folks' place to help with their annual branding.

There are still many ranching traditions alive and well in the West, and branding is one. This involves gathering the cattle on horseback, putting them in a branding pen, and putting our particular brand on them as a way of proving ownership. A few days later, we would turn them out to summer pasture.

Mom was bustling around as usual, trying to be everywhere all at once: in the kitchen cooking for the branding crew, making her way to the pen to make sure everything was set, and checking that the coffee was hot for cold cowboys.

I was struck by how selfless my mom was and what a servant's heart she had — putting everyone else's needs above her own. She loved others deeply.

## A SUDDEN, HEARTBREAKING LOSS

A few days after returning home, I noticed several missed calls and one voicemail from my dad. As I listened to his voice, my heart just knew my mom was gone.

It's crazy how quickly life changed. That morning, my precious mother woke up early, had her quiet time and a cup of coffee, fed my dad breakfast, caught her horse, and proceeded to spend the day like so many others before, working cattle beside her husband. She sorted the calves from the cows as we loaded them onto semi-trucks and hauled them to summer pasture.

My Mom died instantly when her horse fell backward, landing on her.

I moved in slow motion for days. Numbed by it and yet experiencing a raw and deep ache. It felt like my heart was breaking, as if a fist was around it, squeezing the life out of me.

A small part of me wanted to succumb to the feeling of loss and join my mom in heaven. I longed to go to bed, pull the covers over my head, and ignore the world. At the same time, I needed to stay busy and distracted.

The days, weeks, and months that followed were full of uncertainty, anxiety, and deep sadness. I didn't know who I was without my mom. My whole life, I valued the identity of being "Jody White's daughter." Her steadfast love and faith were my anchor.

What would I do without her? How would I face life's challenges without her there to guide me with her wisdom and grace? I struggled to read the Bible or pray. I couldn't concentrate. I found myself skipping church because I would weep at the first worship song. I wasn't angry at God, but I was angry at my mother for leaving.

I was tired of trying to be the strong one as she had been for so long. I just wanted to be alone in my grief.

## ALLOWING GOD TO HEAL MY PAIN

Those closest to me wouldn't let go. They held onto me with a tenacious love. I thought talking about my loss would only bring more pain. But I found the presence of loved ones soothed my jagged edges of grief.

Slowly, I got back in the saddle and got to work.

While moving cattle at our ranch one day, I was overwhelmed with God's love and felt covered in it. In the wide-open spaces and under the clear, blue Wyoming sky — doing what my mother and I both loved so much — I realized God's love had never left me. Like one of my mother's handmade quilts, I felt God cover and wrap me in comfort, peace, and security.

I recalled a verse from Deuteronomy 31:8, "And the Lord, he is the one who goes before you. He will be with you, he will not leave you nor forsake you; do not fear nor be dismayed." The steadfastness of God's love was even more tangible.

Growing up on a ranch, I learned nothing is ever wasted. Every animal and blade of grass is cared for and cultivated to grow into something useful. God doesn't waste anything. He doesn't waste pain or tragedy, suffering or grief. He cares for and cultivates us.

I now see how God used my grief to refine and strengthen me. He gave me a deeper appreciation for life and a desire to love others well, knowing it can be gone in a moment. And through my pain, he gave me compassion for those who grieve.

My mom is gone, but I will see her again. Until then, God remains with me and is my true source of wisdom and guidance.

# WHEN I SECOND-GUESSED GOD

## BY LYNNE MODRANSKI

In 2002, several southern churches invited me to sing. My husband, Steve, and I were three days into the week-long concert tour when my daughter called to announce her pregnancy.

In an instant, the distance between our hotel room in Nashville and our home in eastern Ohio widened. Just that morning, we'd prayed for our grandchildren yet to come, never imagining the first would arrive in less than eight months.

As I shared my music and message in four more churches throughout Alabama and Mississippi, I announced we were grandparents. Though it would be months before we met the wee one, we believed the tiny form was already our grandchild.

Our lives were full of joy as we planned a baby shower and bought a crib. At the time, Steve pastored a church about two hours from our daughter, but God had already scheduled a move. Three months into her pregnancy, we discovered we'd be leading a new church just ten minutes from our new grandbaby in Steubenville, Ohio. We were thrilled.

In May, our daughter's doctor decided it would be best if she induced labor prior to the due date. They chose a date in the middle of June. And for three weeks, I fumed.

I wanted them to wait on God's timing. It would be different if she carried long past 40 weeks or experienced complications. From my perspective, convenience seemed to be the only reason for this induction, as scheduling births kept the doctor from being called out in the middle of the night.

Daily I poured my soul out to God. I cried out to him to stop this doctor. Worried about my daughter and her baby, I followed the advice of 1 Thessalonians 5:17 and "prayed continually" for more than two weeks.

## THE BIG DAY

The final week of waiting saw my prayers change. Rather than giving my Heavenly Father creative ideas on how to protect my daughter and unborn grandchild, I turned my pleas into praise and began to tell God I trusted him to take care of my loved ones.

I truly believed God would allow my daughter to carry this baby and deliver without being induced. However, when the sunny June morning rolled around, I resigned myself to the fact that the doctor won.

Steve went to the hospital early to offer support before heading to help his dad fix a roof. I would go a bit later. After all, induction takes forever, and our son-in-law didn't need us hanging around for hours.

I'd just gotten out of the shower when my husband called with a change of plans. He told me my daughter would have an emergency cesarean delivery.

Every worst-case scenario played in my mind. I was certain the induction had gone wrong. Worry drove me to prayer, and I reminded myself God was bigger than emergencies.

I arrived at the hospital just as they'd gotten my daughter stable enough for surgery. There was time for only a quick hug before they whisked my first baby girl away. I couldn't tell her how much I loved her and the tiny one I'd not met.

The 30-minute wait stretched on forever. I had too much nervous energy to sit, and I'm not a natural crier, so there was no release in tears. I wavered between fear and faith as I prayed silently and listened to Steve and my son-in-law's parents share the events of the morning.

My daughter's plight had nothing to do with the induction. They'd never given her Pitocin, the drug that started the labor process. Before the staff could administer the IV, my daughter's blood pressure had plummeted, and she had passed out. The placenta had torn away from the uterine wall.

Had she not already been in the hospital when it happened, we probably would have lost our daughter and our grandson.

## GOD'S ULTIMATELY IN CONTROL

As the excitement of the morning unfolded, I remembered my prayers of the past two weeks. Relief filled my heart.

I had begged God to cancel the appointment for inducing. Yet the Almighty had bigger plans. I thought about the Sovereign getting Mary and Joseph to Bethlehem at just the right time. The world didn't need a census, but prophecy demanded Jesus be born in David's city.

In the same way, my Redeemer used a doctor who preferred planned births to get my daughter exactly where she needed to be at the right moment. Her doctor may have scheduled Pitocin, but our Creator scheduled a miracle.

From the time her blood pressure stabilized until we were introduced to our grandson, everything went smoothly. When my son-in-law brought out the 6-pound bundle, four grandparents and three aunts waited to meet him.

Our daughter would need a little extra help at home for a week or so, but she'd be fine. I was so relieved — and thankful.

My faith in Jesus grew. He overlooked my doubts and gave us a huge blessing. I learned to trust. My Father's words from Isaiah 55:9 came alive: "As the heavens are higher than the earth, so are my ways higher than your ways and my thoughts than your thoughts."

# HOW A MISCARRIAGE FORCED ME TO BE BRUTALLY HONEST WITH GOD

## BY KERRAH E. FABACHER

My doctor couldn't find the heartbeat.

We had already heard our baby's heartbeat four weeks before this appointment, but all my doctor could hear this time was silence. A silence that felt suffocating.

I had a lump in my throat that kept me silent, too. I saw my baby — my first baby — for the last time. My sweet, still, silent baby. I had to say goodbye before I could even say hello.

The procedure to "remove the baby" was scheduled. I was too far along to try to "pass the baby" on my own. It would be too traumatic, so we had to do the surgical procedure.

I went with my husband to an outpatient surgery center near New Orleans. I was hungry, scared, and brokenhearted. They prepared me for the procedure, and when they gave me the anesthesia, I felt a wave of panic. By the time I woke up, my baby would no longer be a part of me. She would be gone forever.

Numbness set in after I cried. A numbness that kept me from feeling anything at all. Emotionally, I felt dead.

## THE BROKENNESS THAT FOLLOWED

I spent the week after the procedure at home, mainly in my bed, alone. I did not go to any graduate school classes, and I did not go to work. I could not be around anyone. Some beautiful souls brought me food and flowers, but I had nothing to give in return.

When I finally started to feel, the anger and grief and sadness and confusion came in waves, the kind of waves that hurricanes bring. Strong and overpowering.

I had barely any emotional or physical energy to pray, but when I did, my prayers were shallow and inauthentic. I said things I felt I was supposed to say, such as:

"God, you are in control. I trust you."

"God, maybe it was not the right time."

"God, you are still good."

I didn't feel like I believed any of the things I said to God. If I looked long and hard at the condition of my heart, I knew I was angry with him. And confused. And full of doubt and fear.

"Where are you, God? I don't feel you near me."

"Why did you take my baby from me?"

"What did I do to deserve this pain?"

"Do you even love me?"

I sat on the old carpeted floor of my bedroom with tears streaming down my face, and I looked over at my worn Bible and knew I needed to tell him how I felt.

Something in me knew that if I did not tell God how I was honestly feeling and thinking, my relationship with him would be stuck in a state of dishonesty. I would be wearing a mask in the presence of a God who already knew me. And that would prevent him from fully accessing my heart to be able to start healing me.

I remembered passages in the Bible and Jesus crying out with tears during prayer. I decided that if what I knew about prayer were true, then it must be OK for me to tell God how I felt.

Early one morning, unable to sleep, I knew I needed to deal with what was going on in my heart. I decided to lay aside my mask of what I thought a good church girl was supposed to be. I did not want to be gentle or nice or faith-filled. I did not want to say things to God that I did not mean. I just wanted to be honest. So I told him.

I got up and went into our little office so I would not wake up my husband. I sat on an old blue futon. I took a deep breath and reached for a pen. I got my journal and started writing as fast as I could. Anything that came to mind came out on that paper.

"God, where are you?"

"Why would you give her life, a heartbeat, and then take it?"

"I am so angry with you, God. I don't even know if I believe in you right now."

"Will I ever be a mom?"

"Do you even love me?"

I was so vulnerable and honest, more than I had ever been in my life. When I was finished, I slammed the journal shut and threw it across the room. My tears broke free. I cried on that blue futon until exhaustion set in.

I just kept begging for God to hear me.

## AN ANSWERED PRAYER

After lying on that futon, my eyes tired of the tears, I felt a peace flood over me. It was as if I could hear God say to me, "It's OK to be angry and confused. I never left you, and I never will. I am so sorry your baby is not with you. I am weeping with you. I promise she is here with me, safe. She did not get to know you, but she knows me. And you will be a mother again."

I still felt broken and would continue to grieve, but I walked out of that room with hope. I trusted in a God that welcomed my cries and anger and doubt, a God who was compassionate and kind.

My authenticity, vulnerability, and honesty developed a deep connection from my heart to God's. By spilling it all at his feet, I allowed myself to be fully known. It was one of the bravest decisions I had ever made.

At that moment, I realized it was OK for me to tell God how I felt. He wanted me to be honest, and he listened and spoke truth into my broken heart, a truth that healed me.

Sharing my doubts and fears and sadness with God is what he wanted. These prayers are just as important as the prayers of praise and adoration and thanksgiving I learned growing up.

Prayers of anger are just as holy. God hears, and he sees. He can handle what I have to say.

God loves me, and he loves my baby. He never stopped.

# WRESTLING WITH FAITH: WHEN BEING GOOD ISN'T GOOD ENOUGH

## BY JULIANA GORDON

I was a prize-winning Christian. Our local Christian radio station had a booth at the Los Angeles County Fair back in the '80s, and they sponsored a Bible trivia contest. I answered an impressive amount of questions for a 10-year-old, prepared by many years of attending Sunday school and reading Bible storybooks.

I am not sure what I won — maybe a Christian record album? — but I was sure proud of myself.

I was proud of myself in other ways, too. Our home was tucked away in a suburb of Los Angeles, in the San Fernando Valley. There was trouble to be found, but I didn't go looking for it, and it didn't seem to make its way into our home or the parochial schools I attended.

I felt secure in my loving family, not worried about the problems I would see in the after-school specials they showed on TV. I loved pleasing my parents, teachers, and other adults with good grades and behavior. I had accepted Jesus into my heart while I was in preschool, and I believed there was nothing more I needed to do to grow my faith.

As a kid, I stretched the truth to stay out of trouble, stole bites from my sister's Easter candy, and was a shallow friend at times. But I didn't think it was a big deal because it wasn't the "bad" sins my church spent a lot of time warning us against.

As I moved through school, I racked up certificates at award ceremonies. I earned the highest score in my school for the PSAT, a college readiness exam. In high school, my friends and I didn't swear or drink, but I would indulge in gossip. I would judge without compassion. And I would harbor bitterness and unforgiveness.

I figured I was fine, though. I believed I was a good Christian.

## ATTENDING COLLEGE, DRIFTING AWAY FROM CHURCH

In the '90s, I graduated from a well-respected Christian high school in a suburb of Los Angeles. And I drifted away from church.

I lived at home and commuted to the local state university for college. It was so different from my high school and church community. The school was known for its free-thinking, humanistic views — being rather dismissive of the divine — but it also had stellar academics and was close to home, so I enrolled.

I started college in the business program, but I later changed to English with an emphasis in creative writing. Many of my classmates assumed no one there believed in God, so I cringed when I heard their careless, hurtful words about God, Jesus, and religion. The campus felt lonely with no one on "my side."

I hid my beliefs and kept quiet with my classmates and professors. I wanted good grades, and I wanted to be accepted. Without affirmation of my Christian beliefs and without encouragement from other Christians, I found my faith wavering.

By the time I was in my early 20s, I wondered who I was and if my faith was really a part of me. Classmates and professors were making arguments that assumed there wasn't a God, and I simmered in my doubts.

## WRESTLING WITH DOUBTS

My growing anxiety over my beliefs — and concerns about what I wanted to be when I finally "grew up" — pushed me to reach out to my childhood friend Sarah. We decided to go to church together. It was the same church building I attended as a child, but it felt different.

The college pastor welcomed everyone who wanted to learn more about the Christian faith, and he answered questions about the doubts I had. I connected with other believers who were also growing in their faith. It felt as if Jesus reintroduced himself to me, guiding me as I sorted out what I had learned or assumed about him growing up.

I learned that my own goodness would never be good enough to save me. I memorized Ephesians 2:8-9, which says: "For by grace you have been saved through faith. And this is not your own doing; it is the gift of God, not a result of works, so that no one may boast."

My heart was filled with hope as God changed my life. He showed me I could not depend on myself and that my own self-righteousness does not justify me. Before, I thought I was so much better than the "obvious" sinners, but my pettiness, my unkind words, and my selfishness made me a sinner, too. I also needed salvation I could not provide.

When I slipped into my old patterns and habits, God showed me I could confess and be forgiven. And he showed me a new way. God provided new friends to walk beside me, and he gave me mentors who shaped how I view the ministry I'm still part of today.

More than 20 years later, I am so thankful for my difficulty in college. God used my experience attending such an unaccepting place to grow my faith. Instead of trying to earn a spot in the non-existent "Christian Hall of Fame," I am reminded to check my self-righteousness. Only God can save me.

It's OK to doubt, and it's OK to wrestle with my faith. Now I seek wise counsel and address my questions sooner. I pray with trusted friends, and I don't allow doubts to fester. When I do have questions, God reminds me he is always with me and I can trust him.

I will never be good enough, but that's OK because God is.

# FOLLOWING A CALL TO SERVE IN THE MILITARY

## BY ANDY WALTERS

**M**y son cried so hard when I boarded the plane. It was heartbreaking, leaving my family for almost eight weeks, but I knew it was something I needed to do.

After I landed at the San Antonio Airport, I saw the fold-up tables where drivers were taking poor, scared youth off to the unknowns of basic training.

I walked toward the table, more than a decade older than the 18- and 19-year-olds nearby. I had enlisted in the U.S. Air Force National Guard at age 31, following a call that took me years to answer.

I tried not to show my anxiety about what was ahead as I approached. But I was afraid, too. I was scared of being away from my two boys, the strain it would place on our family, and how hard it would be.

I didn't join the Air Force when I was 18, like my best buddy, because something growing up had made me hate the military. Honestly, I think it was my parent's fear.

One of my regrets is rudely telling a recruiter I had no interest in a career of picking up dead bodies. That's where my mind was in 2000.

Then the Sept. 11, 2001, attacks happened, and I felt a call for the first time. It's hard to describe. I felt a push from God, a calling, and a duty to serve my country. But I didn't act on it.

I was starting a life with a good woman, which grew into a promising career, a house, endless opportunities, and then before we knew it, kids. I was in full family mode and loved it. But the calling continued to nag at me. God's whisper to serve.

## FOLLOWING THE CALL

Soon after 9/11, my brother was commissioned into the U.S. Marines. He cleared the way for me, as all good older brothers do. Finally, on March 3, 2012, I decided it was now or never. I prayed and signed the Air Force contract with faith that it was the right thing to do.

The first morning of basic training sucked. So did the rest of the mornings. I had left a well-established career, a wife, kids, and a dog — the American Dream — for screaming drill sergeants and endless formations.

As soon as they found out I was "old," they put me in charge of a bunch of crying, fresh-out-of-high school, first-time-away-from-mommy boys. Some of these boys didn't know how to address a letter! Lucky for them, this "old guy" was there.

The weeks dragged on, and I learned the game. I missed my youngest son's first birthday and my oldest son's fifth birthday. The irony didn't escape me: I gave away my freedom so I could fight for freedom.

My military career has not been easy. I deployed to Kuwait and missed my sons' birthdays again. I went through a divorce, and I had to start over.

But God met me in the desert of Kuwait, just as he met Israel in the desert as he led them to the promised land. It was a lonely time being away from home. And I was recovering from the emotional toil of a divorce that separated our family, something I swore I'd never do.

During the long nights after duty, I wondered where I would live when I returned home or how I would parent two boys alone. I would call them when the sun was setting in Kuwait and rising in Iowa.

## GOD'S IN CONTROL

God never left me, and in many ways, the deployment removed me from the daily pains of divorce and allowed me time and space to heal. I met men and women serving overseas I'd never have otherwise met. And I led a Bible study, which deepened my faith.

Just as God provided for Israel with daily manna, he provided for my daily needs. After I returned home, I bought a house that had been on the market for months. I'm still not sure how I didn't see it while searching online overseas, or how it didn't sell before I returned home.

And I met a woman who'd been part of my group of church friends since she moved to Iowa a few years before. All our friends knew us and assumed we knew each other, but we didn't meet until after I returned from Kuwait and bought my house. I wouldn't have been ready to meet her any earlier.

God has blessed me. He has been with me through the ups and downs. I'm getting married this spring, raising two amazing boys, and starting a life with a beautiful, faith-filled woman.

When I answered God's calling, he was with me through the journey. He knew the challenges I would face, and he provided for me. He took me to places I couldn't imagine and grew me in unexpected ways.

I made myself available, and God walked in front of me, paving the way and preparing blessings I could not see.

# IF GOD IS BIGGER THAN DEATH, THEN GOD IS BIGGER THAN CANCER

## BY ELYSE WEBB

It was mid-morning, and I was riding in the passenger seat of my dad's red pickup truck. The sun was shining, old blues tunes were playing, and the necessary "road trip snack bag" was resting between my dad and me.

We merged onto I-80 as I placed my feet on the dashboard. It was Aug. 6, 2010, and I was mentally prepared for six long hours in a car with my father. Right before I took my first of many naps, he asked me to call and let my mom know we were on the road, heading back to Chicago after my first official college visit.

I was not on the phone for more than a minute when I knew something was wrong. Long somber sighs filled the space as my mom spoke the words.

"Grandma has cancer. Stage 4. The worst it can be."

I remember hearing those words as I stared blankly ahead as white lines on the highway passed. As she continued to talk, tears started to involuntarily roll down my cheeks, my voice shook, and my breathing quickened.

I started sobbing uncontrollably. This was the first time anyone in my family received this type of news. It was also the first time I saw my father cry.

We sat in silence on the side of the highway together.

Within the next two years, five other cancer diagnoses would come with a vengeance into my life. At that moment, cancer became the enemy. And the enemy brought what I believed was the absolute worst thing there was in this world. Death.

At 17 years old, I was filled with fury: I was angry at the God I had grown up believing in. I falsely believed he bestowed this evil thing upon my family.

During the last few months of high school, I became increasingly aware of other families struggling with cancer diagnosis. When my creative writing teacher asked us to produce a short documentary, I proclaimed: "I am going to create one all about cancer." In comparison, my classmates created lighthearted videos, such as "Everything you need to know about cheese."

Instead, I marched with a mini camcorder to our town's local cancer support center. That day, I interviewed parents, family members, and those with cancer. I asked every person how they remained happy, even after this diagnosis.

## SEARCHING FOR ANSWERS

I ended my day at the support center by interviewing an art therapist who worked with individuals and families impacted by cancer. As she spoke, I searched for a common thread that validated how awful and angry I was feeling.

All I could find? "Love more."

It's the idea that if you love more — more people, your current situation, the everyday mundane — then everything would be OK. But to me, it wasn't the answer.

People around me kept dying, and no one was telling me it was OK to feel anger. They told me to be positive and have faith, but I thought that was a false hope.

I did not know what to grasp onto. I did not know what books to read. I did not know how to fix the brokenness. I didn't know what to say when people asked me how I was feeling. Instead of confronting it, I pushed my anger away and hid it.

One night after a grueling day at work, I sat at my kitchen island to finish dinner. My roommate and I chatted about our day when I received a phone call from my dad, and I was glad he did so I could tell him about my car's oil light.

When I finally took a breath, I asked, "So, how are you and Mom?" My father took a deep breath, and his voice began to shake. "I am sorry to have to tell you this over the phone, but Grandma died today."

The anger resurfaced. I wanted to travel back in time to before my father told me. But I knew I couldn't. After crying together once again, I collected myself and went to my room to process my next steps: When to tell my boss, what to pack in a bag, and when to travel back home.

But first, I grabbed my Bible. It was a brown Bible I had purchased five years earlier, which was now filled with pencil markings, random notes, and prayers. I flipped through the pages hoping to grasp onto something bigger than me — something bigger than anger.

Days later, I traveled home with that same Bible in hand. I added one of my grandma's handwritten letters to me, a photograph of her from my childhood, and tabbed the first reading I was to read at her funeral.

There was not a single dry eye as I stood preaching God's word about her and her legacy as a noble wife, mother, and grandmother.

## EMBRACING GOD'S PEACE

Coming back to West Des Moines, Iowa, after weeks of traveling to and from Chicago, I continued my routine of attending my normal church service at 9:15 a.m. I sat in my usual spot with my usual church crew.

That morning, our worship leader opened the service with a song I'd never heard before. As most do, I pretended to know the words and swayed to the music.

A flood of emotion poured out of me. It was this overwhelming feeling as I sang the lyrics — "Take me wider than the atmosphere, where east and west just disappear" — and I began to remember my grandma.

I began to imagine where she was now. I began to feel as if I was the only person in the church. The background noise faded, and I zeroed in on the moment. I felt this strong presence of her, but also of God.

The moment took me away from the chaos around me and centered me in the oddest way. I was feeling a million different things: sadness, wonder, loneliness, tragedy, and awe. But not one ounce of anger. Not one.

The emotion I had carried with me for eight years was gone. I thought if God was bigger than death, then God was bigger than cancer.

I was filled with peace.

On May 2, 2018, my grandma died. Today, I have no doubt I will see her again in heaven, and I can only imagine what she will say to me.

# THE CHAINS OF ADDICTION WERE BROKEN

## BY JON THOMPSON

In 2015, I had a job I enjoyed, which hasn't happened very often in my life. Before, I was driving a truck and working 70 hours a week, so this job was a blessing. I was able to get off the road. I spent more time at home.

Then in 2016, the company I worked for reorganized, so I went from management to a grunt to a nobody. And during this process, I didn't realize how much this was affecting me emotionally and mentally.

Up to this point, I mainly dealt with my emotions and anxiety by acting out with unhealthy behaviors. So that's what I did until 2017, when it blew up.

Everything that I had been dealing with for the last 40-some years was actually an addiction. I had no idea.

### CONFRONTING ADDICTION

I didn't know what to do, so I went into cleanup mode. I did everything I could. I signed up for Celebrate Recovery, which guided me through a biblical approach to recovery, and I found a therapist. I went to a small group. I did everything I thought I was supposed to do to help fix me.

I knew if I didn't fix this problem, I was gonna lose my marriage, my kids, and my grandkids.

I kept on checking off boxes in my 12-step class, thinking, "Hey, I'm doing good."

I started The Ultimate Journey, and that was the game changer. That's where I met the Holy Spirit in a way I'd never imagined. He took me back to my childhood, and I was able to reconnect to my inner child, to be able to understand what happened to me as a kid and be able to understand where Jesus was.

Then in September 2017, it blew up again. I had not been sober for seven months. I was still acting out, and I was still doing all my old behaviors. I just hid it better.

## SONGS OF PRAISE FILLED THE CAR

Things started going better, and it's been better.

Earlier this year, I was driving back from St. Cloud, Minnesota, and I was sitting in silence. I realized that the silence was not helping at all, so I plugged my phone into the car.

I found one song after another, and I had a phenomenal worship service with Jesus. He put together a playlist for me, just song after song after song. The words rang out:

"I am free."

"The chains are broken."

"I am loved."

Everything I had been wanting. Finally, the Zach Williams song, "Fear is a Liar," came on. The chorus struck me: "Let your fire fall and cast out all my fears / Let your fire fall / Your love is all I feel."

The Holy Spirit fell in the car. I just sat there, and at that very moment, something struck me to the core. Nothing like that had happened to me before.

I had total, unbelievable peace.

I knew that if anything happened to me at the moment, I was going to be alright. I had a deep understanding, a deep feeling inside. I understood God loved me.

I don't have a job right now, but that's OK. I know I'm going to be OK because I have unshakable peace.

I want to give glory to God for everything he has done for me because if it wasn't for him, I wouldn't be here right now. And I want to give him thanks for that.

# HOW GOD RECONNECTED ME WITH A LOST LOVED ONE

## BY VANESSA MAY

Shortly after the COVID-19 pandemic began, I called my older friend Milly and left her messages, but I did not hear back. I started to worry that Milly, at 86, had contracted the virus and passed away — and no one thought to let me know.

Milly lives in a nursing home near Dallas, Texas, but I live in Des Moines, Iowa. We stayed in touch with our cell phones. I have known Milly all my life. Since my mother passed, Milly has been a mother figure to me, and we have fun, sweet conversations on the phone about grandchildren.

Milly is prone to falls, so I tried to call often. The last time I talked to her was after a fall. She was very confused and crying throughout the call.

In June 2020, I tried to call Milly but couldn't get through. Then I tried Milly's daughter, but her number had changed. I was becoming despondent, thinking I had missed an opportunity to tell Milly I loved her once again. I did what she and I do frequently. I prayed.

I asked God to let me know how she was — either way.

### RECONNECTING: DIVINE INTERVENTION

On this particular day, I was contemplating calling Milly's nursing home to see if they would at least give me Milly's son's number. I wanted to know if she was OK.

My husband and I have home-based businesses with two landlines used mainly for faxing, which, up until a couple of days earlier, were not working after a storm. Once the lines were fixed, there were dozens of messages I had not yet heard. Most of the calls are telemarketers, so I tend to put off listening to them. I clear them when I think of it.

When I looked at the blinking lights this time, I decided to check them after I got back from the post office. Then one of the phone lines rang. I decided not to pick it up — until I noticed the number on the caller ID had an area code that looked familiar.

A thought went through my mind: "Answer it!"

So I did, hesitantly. I was dreading the telemarketer's typical "Do not hang up!"

Then I heard a familiar voice say, "Vanessa?"

It was Milly!

I was flooded with relief. She was OK!

Milly was asking if she had the right number, which I confirmed it was, and then she said something to someone on her end and asked if she could call me back.

I panicked a little but then realized I had her new number on the caller ID.

After quite a while, she called me back. She explained they had moved her to a facility in a different town to recover from her last fall and had put her chair and personal things in storage.

Her phone was locked up in storage with all her numbers on it.

How did she call me, then?

## AN ANSWERED PRAYER

Milly told her nurse she needed to call me, but she didn't have my number and could not remember my married name. She knew I lived in Des Moines with my husband John.

The nurse Googled the name "Vanessa" in Des Moines.

Then she read the Google list to Milly, but Milly did not recognize any names until the name of my business popped up.

Milly said, "Yes! That's the one!"

I was amazed! I never talk with Milly about my business. Our conversation is usually about bingo games and funny things grandkids say and do.

"Man, it's a good thing I don't live in New York!" I thought.

At that moment, I realized God had orchestrated our connection. There simply is no other explanation. There were too many variables. There were too many unknowns.

God's timing is impeccable.

The phone lines were working, Milly had the right nurse to help her, and I was home and answered a phone call I normally would send to voicemail.

I felt renewed in my faith. There is no doubt in my mind God listens and answers prayers.

# AS I FACED MY WORST FEARS AS A MOTHER, I LEARNED TO TRUST GOD

## BY CARRIE M. HOLT

My husband and I were startled awake in the early morning hours as we heard our 5-year-old son's night nurse calling. An anxious feeling grew in my stomach. Something was wrong with our son, Toby.

In a matter of minutes, I was on my feet and acknowledging one of my worst fears: Toby was having his first seizure. This wasn't our first trip to the hospital in an ambulance. We were more familiar than most with the hospital in Columbus, Ohio.

In late 2006, Toby was born with a condition called Spina Bifida. He was born with an open hole in his back when the bones of the spinal column didn't close around his spinal cord, causing damaged nerves, muscles, and paralysis.

Two weeks later, his situation worsened when he went into respiratory failure, the result of complications due to a malformation in his brain. Two months later, we brought home a medically fragile baby with a tracheostomy, a ventilator, a feeding tube, and home nursing care. This was rare for our son's condition but not completely unexpected.

### FACING MY WORST FEAR

Five years later, we had been through some pretty scary medical scenarios, but I feared seizures the most. Maybe it was my lack of control, the medications used to treat them, or trepidation over it hurting our son mentally, but seizures were scary.

Most people have a bucket list. I, as a special needs mom, have an "unbucket" list of events I never want my son to experience. Seizures were on that list.

After we arrived at the hospital, his second seizure began. It lasted four to six hours, leaving doctors puzzled about how to stop it. His body became so fatigued it couldn't shake anymore, even though he was convulsively seizing. I was devastated.

I began to wonder if God had missed this. Had he been looking the other way? We felt completely blindsided. I felt forsaken and alone. Didn't God know we had already been through so much? Shouldn't we get a free pass on future suffering?

After all, my husband and I had already proven we were faithful. We went to church, led a Bible study, and sent our kids to a Christian school.

We weren't angry about what life had dealt us the previous five years. Hadn't we proven our faithfulness — so nothing bad should happen to us anymore?

Then the fear set in. I feared Toby wouldn't wake up. I feared he wouldn't be the same mentally. Toby lost the ability to speak when he was six weeks old with his tracheotomy surgery. I didn't hear him say the word "Mama" until he was almost three. I feared he wouldn't be able to tell me he loved me.

## I PUT MY TRUST IN GOD

I felt sick and decided to go for a walk. As I paced the sidewalks outside the children's hospital, I prayed. I cried. I ranted. I grieved.

Then I checked my phone. There was the encouragement I needed through the texts of friends: "God knew this was going to happen." "He prepared us for this moment." "He is with us now." "He never left."

It still took some time to fight the fears and questions of what was happening, but I kept going back to read those truths.

Just because our circumstances had changed didn't mean God's character had. He was still the same loving, trustworthy Heavenly Father who had a purpose and plan. He would walk through this with us. I breathed deeply, cried, prayed, and chose to focus on the moment in front of me.

The next afternoon, as a nurse was caring for Toby, his eyes began to flutter open. I rushed to his bedside. As we asked him questions, he shook his head no, even though he could barely hold his head up. He tried to smile.

I was relieved, grateful, and then joyous. He was going to recover.

By the time our son was 14, he experienced nearly 60 surgeries. His seizures impacted my life in particular.

Past difficulties don't negate future walks of sorrow.

Each time they wheel Toby's bed into yet another surgery, I face similar fears. My son and I always pause in the hospital hallway to hug tightly and share words of comfort.

Each time I wonder: Is this it? Will he wake up from this one?

Then Toby reminds me, using the voice he was blessed to gain at age 3: "God's got me. He's with me, Mom."

# GOD ANSWERED MY PRAYERS WHILE I WAS GIVING BIRTH WITHOUT MY FAMILY

## BY TALEIZA CALLOWAY-APPLETON

Growing up, I used to tell my mother I did not think I was strong enough for childbirth. After all the stories I had read and movies I had seen, I just did not think I could do it. The pain of labor terrified me.

Well, God showed me just how strong I was through the arrival of my baby girl, Reima, in the middle of the global pandemic of 2020.

Childbirth wasn't new to me. My oldest son Levi was born on the first day of spring in March 2014. My mother and husband were there when he arrived to offer support and love and celebrate his birth.

My middle child Royce was born two weeks early in November 2017. Again, my husband was with me, holding my hand and praying with me as I welcomed him into the world.

We live in the Bay Area of California and we were in lockdown. The governor had issued a stay-at-home order, which limited travel for "non-essential workers." I knew the birth of my third child, my sweet Reima, would be so different. I feared the idea of no one being there to calm me if she had a birth defect. I worried there would be no one there to encourage me if I had to have a cesarean delivery.

### GOD'S NUDGE TO PREPARE

On May 31, 2020, I randomly said to my husband: "I feel the need to pack my bag for the hospital."

I was nine months pregnant with Reima. We had often talked about how the delivery would go as we were sheltering in place due to the pandemic. Hospitals were limiting how many people could be in the delivery room. Waiting rooms were closed.

I prayed things would be better by the time Reima arrived.

On June 1, I woke up excited to begin the week. It was the start of the final countdown to meeting Reima and Levi's last week of kindergarten.

However, Reima had other plans as I began to have contractions. I called the doctor, and she said I needed to head to the hospital. My husband had left for work about 30 minutes prior. I could not believe the timing of everything, but God had prepared me. My hospital bag was already packed.

My husband came home and took me to the hospital. I waved goodbye to my children and told them I loved them. I said, "Mommy will see you soon and with your new sister!"

I was already anxious about going to the hospital solo. My husband and I put on our face masks, and he walked me into the emergency room entrance. A nurse greeted us with a wheelchair, and then I hugged my husband goodbye.

I know God was with me in the hospital. He helped me hold back tears as I watched my husband leave. He helped me smile at my children in the car — even though I was scared about the experience I was walking into. I felt so alone.

I still praise God that no one cried during the drop-off because I would not have been able to handle that!

## PRAYING THROUGH THE DELIVERY

God helped ease my anxiety about the COVID-19 test results as I waited to be transferred to a birthing room. He helped me push through the pain as I delivered my daughter in a room full of strangers.

"We're here for you," said Nurse Sumi as we waited for the test results.

Sumi also held my hand as I got my epidural. She told me, "You rocked it!" when the anesthesiologist had to insert the needle in my spine for a second time to reposition it.

Before her shift ended, Sumi said she would come back in the morning so she could meet Reima. She returned the next day as promised. I will never forget her kindness or those of the other medical providers.

No, they were not my family, but God helped me to lean on them and not focus on who was not there. He made me strong enough to deliver my baby girl alone. And when it was over, I had never felt so brave.

Reima was born Monday, June 1, 2020 — 12 days early. And I had the honor of cutting Reima's umbilical cord, a task my husband did for both of our sons. I am so grateful I had a great team of nurses to care for me and hold my hand as I birthed my daughter.

I have always liked Romans 12:12, "Rejoice in the hope. Endure under tribulation. Persevere in prayer." It speaks to me, often pertains to my life, and provides reassurance.

When I read this verse, I am reminded that when life gets hard, it is important to endure and remember that what I am going through will not last forever.

More than anything, these words remind me that God sees me and hears my prayers. God was there with me. He knows my heart and knows what I can and cannot handle. He heard my prayers for strength to safely deliver my baby and to make it home to my family. For this, I am forever grateful.

# AFTER MY FIRST HUSBAND'S DEATH, GOD'S PLANS FOR MY FUTURE

## BY MARY POTTER KENYON

The kitchen was quiet except for the soft sound of my pen moving across the paper and the intermittent rustling of a newspaper on the other side of the table. Intent on writing, I barely noticed when my husband David rose to refill my coffee cup.

Sensing his gaze, I glanced up, smiling and thanking him for the coffee, then continued writing. When I looked up again a few minutes later, his eyes were still on me with an expression I'd begun seeing more frequently of late: complete and utter adoration.

"What?" I asked, my face warming at the intensity of his look.

"I'm thinking how beautiful you are and talented. You sit there, and all these words just flow out of you."

I hadn't washed my hair, applied makeup, or changed from my ratty pajamas, and my husband found me attractive? He had to be seeing me through the eyes of love.

We had an enviable marriage by March 2012, an easy companionship centered on love, commitment, and putting each other first.

Our relationship hadn't always been that way, which was why it was all the more remarkable in its richness. We were struggling college students when we got married in 1979. The first of our eight children arrived less than a year later.

Bogged down by bills and babies, by our 25th anniversary, I sometimes wondered if ours was a marriage to celebrate. That changed when David was diagnosed with cancer in 2006, and I became his caregiver. For the first time in years, I put him first — and that triggered the difference.

In our relationship, we'd become true partners in life.

"This is what God meant marriage to be," I thought, realizing how lucky I was to share life with my best friend.

## OVERWHELMED BY GRIEF

Within days of that kitchen table exchange, we were headed to the emergency room. David had been experiencing shoulder pain that had moved to his chest.

We were informed he'd experienced several small heart attacks and needed stent surgery. Three days after he came home from the hospital, I found him unresponsive in the recliner. He'd died sometime during the night. It was the day before his 61st birthday.

And just like that, in one swift moment, I was a 52-year-old widow. Four of our children still lived at home, the youngest just eight years old. The grief was overwhelming, and the next few days were a blur. Instinctively, I knew I needed two things: prayer and Bible verses.

I wasn't certain how to find either, but I did know how to write my way through difficult times. I'd penned my way through my husband's cancer treatment; my mother's terminal cancer and death 17 months before; and our five-year-old grandson's cancer diagnosis, treatment, and recent recurrence.

While I'd never learned to study the Bible, I was familiar with many verses, including 1 Thessalonians, on "giving thanks in all things."

Forty-eight hours after my husband's death, I opened a journal and began listing all the things I was grateful for. The 5 ½ years with my husband after his cancer; our revitalized relationship; our children; the siblings who surrounded me like cotton batting; and a modest life insurance policy reinstated just 27 days before.

As I filled three pages that morning, it occurred to me how God had prepared me for the loss of my husband, such as our conversation at the kitchen table.

I devoured devotionals, the Bible, and inspirational and encouraging books by authors who had mourned the loss of a spouse before me. I studied the science of bereavement, believing God designed us to withstand grief. I wanted to know the science behind what the Bible said. I copied passages and quotes in my journal, little pinpricks of hope amid the darkness of grief.

Jeremiah 29:11 stood out the most, becoming my life's verse: "For I know the plans I have for you," declares the Lord, "plans to prosper you and not to harm you, plans to give you hope and a future."

## DISCOVERING GOD'S PLAN FOR THIS SEASON

I'd been David's wife for almost 34 years and a mother for nearly as long. I barely knew who I was outside of those relationships. Though I'd managed to graduate from college, outside of freelance writing and various home businesses, I'd become increasingly isolated: A stay-at-home mom who could barely string two sentences together to talk to the butcher or mailman.

David had been the one to encourage me to branch out and conduct couponing and writing workshops for local community colleges. He'd sat at the back of the room to watch, marveling how I'd come alive in front of an audience.

With David's sudden death, I was thrust into a state of stillness I'd never experienced as a busy mother. It was in that stillness I found God. Though I continued the workshops, I gave myself the gift of a year to grieve and delve into God's word before I looked for work outside my home.

I followed the leading of the Holy Spirit as I navigated those first 12 months of widowhood, spending hours on my couch, reading, writing, and praying. For the first time in my life, I learned to truly listen and discern God's answers to my prayers.

Ten months after my husband's death, my newfound faith was put to the test when we discovered my grandson's cancer was terminal. He had less than a year to live.

Because I needed to understand how God works through our grief, I knew others in my church must need it too. One Sunday, a few days before the first anniversary of David's death, I stood in front of our church congregation and announced a Bible study, and I briefly shared my story. Fifty people signed up. We met for two years before breaking off into a group of seven that met in my home.

I yearned to help others, to minister to hurting souls through the gift of presence. I took online courses to become a certified grief counselor. I spoke to grief support groups on finding hope and healing, and I founded an annual grief retreat. I eventually found work at a spirituality center where I could freely discuss my faith and God every day.

God did indeed have plans for me, plans for hope and a future I could never have imagined. I discovered a sense of purpose through my broken self, laid bare by grief. When I opened myself to him fully in prayer and learned to listen, I discovered God's direction.

# WHY WE WELCOMED A YOUNG MAN, ABOUT TO BECOME HOMELESS, INTO OUR HOME

## BY DAVID STREGE

While a sophomore in a parochial high school, I thought about becoming a pastor, so I signed up for classes to prepare for seminary. But I didn't get the needed classes, which was an indication that being a pastor was not God's preferred path for me.

I attended Drake University in Des Moines and went into business, but I explored being a pastor again as an adult. I believe all Christians are in ministry, but was I to be a minister? Again, the answer to my prayer was no.

Maybe ten years later, the church we were attending began offering a program to become a pastor. It would train us without the added commitment of seminary. Again, I explored becoming a pastor, but the calling wasn't there. I felt God wanted me on a different path.

As I discussed the decision with God, studied his Word, and sought him in prayer, he showed me his direction — just as he had before.

When our two kids were in high school, for example, we started fostering children. My wife, Jennifer, is brilliant with preschool-aged children; she's able to connect and has a gift for taking care of them. We've since fostered 27 children over the years.

More recently, I felt called to go deeper in my service, to invest my time and resources in new ways.

## PRAYING A SCARY PRAYER

I rarely miss a day of work, and July 10, 2014, was no different. I was about to go to a meeting when my right side fell asleep. From head to toe, I was numb. I could walk, I could talk, but I was numb. I googled the symptoms but didn't find anything. The next day the doctor checked me out and ordered an MRI. I didn't have the symptoms, but he diagnosed me as having had a minor stroke.

I went through physical therapy, and within three months, I was back playing competitive volleyball in the Global Cup finals against Russia. It was as if God said: You need to step up your game.

I spend time each morning in prayer, and shortly after, I decided to open myself to being used by God. I prayed, "I'm here. Whatever you call me to do, show me that path and let me follow it. Use me!"

It's a scary prayer because I didn't know how God was going to call me or how he wanted to use me. Did he want to take me to South Africa?

I felt God was leading me to serve at Wildwood Hills Ranch in St. Charles, Iowa. It serves children who have been victims of abuse or whose family struggles with poverty, drugs, or poor decisions. We were familiar with the challenges because of the foster children we had cared for. I believed we could make a difference.

I started volunteering with the fishing program. I'd be in 90-degree heat, rejigging the poles, and helping kids catch their first fish. Then during the school year, I would teach older kids about personal finance.

Through the program, I got to know a young man who was about to become homeless. He had been in prison for five years and was about to be evicted from his apartment. He was 25, but he didn't know how to drive, and he didn't have a car. I felt God calling us to bring him into our home.

## FOLLOWING GOD

I had so many questions. Was I going down a path I didn't want to go? Was God going to take me into an area I'm not equipped?

Dee came into our home, and God provided. We helped him get a job. We drove him there and back. We taught him to drive and helped him get a license. I have a busy schedule, but my calendar was always free right when I needed it to be in order to help him take the next step.

Dee and I talked about faith. He had made mistakes, and I told him, "I'm not going to judge you. Only God can judge. But I will hold you accountable."

Dee ended up moving out. He fell back into old habits. I haven't heard from him for a while, but he did write me a thank you letter on Father's Day. It was a tearjerker.

My personal approach is to try to solve the problems of the world one person at a time. If I can take this one person and help them get on God's intended path for them, then it's time well spent.

I think about Psalm 119:105 a lot. "Your word is a lamp for my feet, a light on my path." God lays out our whole path for us, but he only shows us the next step. What I know is God provides, in his own way and timing, each step of the way.

# THE GIFT OF MY MOM

## BY KARI SCHULTE

"Your mom has dementia."

When I heard those words from the doctor, my heart sank. I sat expressionless, trying to be strong for my mom. I wasn't surprised. We were already three years into a journey of her being confused. She had difficulty with everyday tasks. I guess I just didn't want to know, or as my husband Rich calls it, "Team Ostrich."

I was filled with questions. How do we figure out the best treatment for her? How do I tell her she can't drive anymore? Where do I start to find a safe place for her to live, not to mention the time to clean out the home she's lived in for 26 years?

I was so scared — for both of us.

We went to the car, and I attempted to gently recap the conversation we just had with the doctor. She had already forgotten the diagnosis. I told her she couldn't drive anymore, and the doctor recommended we start looking for a safe place for her to live. I tried to discuss it with a "we've got this" attitude.

The conversation was so sad. We sat in the car and cried. This was one of those times I needed my mom, but now she needed me more.

I now had a new identity. I was a caregiver. This wasn't the "job" I wanted, but my mom was an only child with little family, and my sister lived out of state. I left a job I enjoyed to take care of the woman who had always been there for me.

I had so many emotions. I was full of anger and frustration. I was overwhelmed and exhausted. I was conflicted about spending so much time with my mom and not my own family. And I was sad. My mom was slipping away.

I tried to educate myself about dementia and Alzheimer's. I read books and attended seminars and support groups. I talked to anyone I could find who had experience with Alzheimer's to help me understand the disease and where we were headed.

With that knowledge, I began to feel empowered about my new role. I had so many new titles: banker, financial advisor, attorney, medical advisor, real estate agent, chauffeur, entertainment director, chef, cleaning lady, pharmacist, and more. Talk about on-the-job training! I learned more in one and a half years than in any corporate training program.

## A YEAR TO REMEMBER

Two weeks before we moved my mom to an independent senior living community, in January of 2018, my husband was diagnosed with early-onset Parkinson's disease. He was 54. We took some time and decided to downsize to a handicap-accessible home. Then in March, I sold my mom's home.

In May, our daughter graduated from college and got a job as a hot dogger for Oscar Mayer, driving the Wienermobile around the country for a year. I was so thankful for the joy God gave us in the middle of a storm.

A few months later, I realized my mom's memory loss was progressing, and she needed to move again, this time to assisted living. As we prepared to move out of the house we had raised our family in for 21 years, the thought of moving us, and my mom, was daunting. I was stressed, which brought on health issues of my own, including extremely high blood pressure.

I knew God was telling me to slow down and take care of myself. I sought ways to reduce my stress. And I prayed. I had faith. In October, we moved into our new home, and five days later, my maternal step-grandmother (my mom's stepmom) passed away. I dreaded the trip to Minnesota with my mom for the funeral but knew I needed to do it.

The 48 hours with her were heart-wrenching. Most of the time, she thought I was her cousin and could not believe I was her daughter. We shed many tears. At one point, she did say, "I'm so glad I know that you're my daughter. I've always liked you."

I thought: Thank you, God, for your humor!

## GOD'S FAITHFULNESS THROUGH THE STORM

So, where is the resolution in this story? As far as my mom's health goes, there probably isn't any. And I'm still a fairly stressed-out mess. But you know what? We're still standing!

Three years ago, I didn't think there was any way I could handle the role of caregiver. God was in the details. He faithfully showed up when we needed him. He showed up in my mom's awesome sense of humor. He showed up when my mom told me a detailed story about her youth (for the 80th time) by reminding me she was still there.

She may not remember things from minute to minute, hour to hour, or day to day, but God is reminding me that she lives in the now, which reminds me how I should live.

God's unconditional love has shown up in so many people he has put in my path to help me, such as friends, strangers, physicians, counselors, my Tuesday bible study gals, my couples small group, my mom's friends, relatives, my dad, my sister, my kids, and my husband.

I have friends who say, "I don't know how you do it." You know what? I don't either, but I do know now it's all in God's hands.

For my birthday, Rich and I picked my mom up and met my dad to celebrate. My mom didn't really remember it was my birthday leading up to that day, but she handed me a card during dinner.

On the inside, she wrote: "You are a very special daughter. I love you so much. Thank you, God, for giving me Kari. Mom"

I was overwhelmed. My mom wasn't talking to me — she was talking to God. The lady who I thought only went to church to socialize was talking to God. She was thanking him for the gift he gave her 56 years ago. Me!

There are days when I think I can't go on as a caregiver, and then God shows up in his perfect timing. My mom's memory is still deteriorating. We recently moved her to memory care, but despite the decline, I thank God for the gift he has given me. The privilege of taking care of my mom.

# FROM HOPELESS TO HOPEFUL WHEN EPILEPSY RAISED ITS UGLY HEAD

## BY JEN NELSON

My youngest son, Michael, has high-functioning autism and epilepsy. When he was five years old, he became fascinated by people doing good things to help others. When we went to church, he immediately noticed ushers and greeters in bright blue shirts.

"How old do you need to be to wear the blue shirt and do that?" Michael said.

My husband Scott noticed a connection card, and following God's nudge, he and Michael joined the hospitality team. My older son Andrew and I would save seats for them each Sunday.

Ushering was such a great way for Michael to practice connecting with others, such as making eye contact, saying good morning, and getting people to smile. He loved his "special spot" for handing out bulletins.

After several months, Michael started asking: "When are you, Mom, and big brother going to usher?" It felt like a "God wink" moment — a time when you stop and think: "That was God, that was the Holy Spirit." So we started ushering as a family and getting more involved at our church.

## FORMING A CHURCH FAMILY

Because we stood in the same greeting spot each Sunday, people started remembering Michael, 11, and Andrew, 14. When they handed out bulletins, many would say: "Thank you, Andrew. Thank you, Michael." At 14, nothing is cool, but I think Andrew secretly enjoyed it.

Michael was diagnosed five years ago with epilepsy. A common symptom of epilepsy is seizures or abnormal activity in the brain. During Michael's seizures, he's not aware of his surroundings, and while he can move or speak, he is confused and unaware of what's going on.

One recent Sunday, Michael had a mild seizure right before ushering. It didn't last very long, he recouped well, and though he wasn't 100%, he still wanted to serve.

On a typical Sunday, Michael might be slow to hand out programs. He might not always smile. Sometimes his hands shake. But people are so kind. We can feel the love of God through God's people.

Over the last few years, we have seen multiple specialists and tried multiple seizure medications. Recently, Michael has been having seizures almost every week. It was a scary time. Between the seizures and the medicine's side effects, we felt frustrated and hopeless. Nothing seemed to work.

After service one Sunday, we stood and talked to family members and our pastor. Andrew noticed Michael having a seizure, and we caught him before he fell. Pastor Ben put his hand on Michael and prayed for him. It was a surreal moment for me. Never have I felt God so much as that moment.

## TRUSTING GOD THROUGH THE STORMS

When someone is experiencing a seizure, the best thing you can do is to keep people safe. And I pray as it's happening and when it's over. I ask God to keep Michael safe. And to keep our family strong. God always has.

There are days when I have doubts. I think, "Will I be able to give it to God?" But I also know the more we give it to God, the more God can work.

Currently, for the first time in a long time, Michael's seizures are controlled, and we have found the right medication. We have a sense of peace, but we also know there will be more storms.

It's been such a journey. I have seen God turn what I once thought was hopeless into something so hopeful. I'm not scared anymore. I know God loves Michael, and he works through Michael to remind me God loves me.

The more I open my eyes to God's work, the more I see his love. Together, we can find joy on the journey.

# TRUSTING GOD AFTER LOSING MY DAD

## BY BETH HAAG

One of the things my mom and I did after my dad passed away was travel. We weren't able to do much traveling in the last two years of my dad's life because, for 25 years, my dad battled an undiagnosed neurodegenerative disorder. He was slowly robbed of his ability to walk, talk, write, and swallow. After he passed away on Dec. 30, 2014, we learned from his autopsy he had multiple system atrophy — often called "Parkinson's on speed."

On April 2, 2016, my parents would have celebrated 50 years of marriage. In honor of that, my mom wanted to take a train trip through the Canadian Rockies. As part of our package, we received free vouchers for the Vancouver Lookout, so we decided to start our day at the tower, which was 553 feet above the city.

A tour guide offered to point out various landmarks and neighborhoods. When she showed us the longest suspension bridge in Western Canada, which is named after two North Shore mountain peaks, I started bawling.

I looked at my mom and said, "You know the Lions Gate story, don't you?"

With tears falling down my face and a shaky voice, I told her and the guide.

When my dad's speech became hard to understand, and he couldn't hear very well, we bought my dad whiteboards to help with communication. Sadly, his writing wasn't much better.

He had scribbled the words "Lions Gate" on one of his whiteboards; he was following the entertainment corporation's stock. I was familiar with it because it's the production group that created one of my all-time favorite TV shows, "Nashville."

As we stood that day looking at the Lions Gate Bridge in Vancouver, the whiteboard in my dad's office still had the words "Lions Gate" on it. Once the tour guide heard the story, she suggested seeing the bridge up close.

There was a Lions Gate Bridge bus stop inside Stanley Park. However, due to a car accident, the park entrance was temporarily closed. When the bus stopped at Prospect Point, we could see the Lions Gate Bridge from the bus. I took a couple of photos, but we didn't get off to explore.

I was disappointed. Deep in my heart, I knew I needed to come back.

## THE ULTIMATE VIEW

To celebrate my 50th birthday, my mom and I returned to Vancouver in October 2017 to attend the Hearties Family Reunion — a weekend with people who are fans of the Hallmark Channel series "When Calls the Heart."

At the reunion, a woman asked if she and her two daughters could sit at our table. When we asked where they were from, we were thrilled to find out Marcy was also from Iowa. In a ballroom full of 450 people, the five Iowans ended up at the same table.

When Marcy mentioned they'd been to Stanley Park, I shared how I wanted to get a picture of the Lions Gate Bridge with me holding a picture of my dad's Lions Gate handwritten sign.

The Sunday after our tour ended, my mom and I ventured into our rented KIA Soul to drive to Stanley Park. We parked and took pictures of me holding a picture of Dad's Lions Gate sign with the bridge behind me.

As we walked on a trail that appeared to go down to the bridge, we saw the lion statutes Marcy had told me about. Then I saw a commemorative plaque: "This table was erected to commemorate the visit of their majesties King George VI and Queen Elizabeth to Vancouver on May 29th, 1939, when their majesties crossed this Lions Gate Bridge."

The bridge was dedicated 12 days after my dad was born.

Coincidence? I don't think so.

I pointed the date out to my mom with tears coming down my face. We hugged.

We started walking on another trail, which took us down a steep hill to the waterfront path. I was concerned about how much walking my 82-year-old mom could handle. We were alone in a foreign country without a clear idea as to where we were heading.

The trees were mammoth and so dense we could no longer see the bridge. I tried to use Google Maps to find the shortest route back to Prospect Point, but without a clear point of reference, the directions didn't help. And my phone battery was quickly dying.

Truth be told, we were lost.

## TRUSTING THE PATH

On a whim, we left the paved path for another trail. As we walked, I kept reminding myself of the "Follow the Cloud" Bible teachings I'd read recently in John Stickl's book. Based on Exodus 13:21-22, the teachings encouraged me to have the courage to trust God. To take the next step without being able to see my destination.

Instead of worrying about being lost, I tried to appreciate all the beauty around me. The fall foliage. The maple leaves twice the size of my mom's hand. The trees made us look like ants when we stood next to them. Once I let go of the worry, I saw people at the top of the hill. I felt instant relief as we returned to civilization.

Then I realized where we were. Our hike had taken us from the waterfront path along the Vancouver Harbor all the way to Stanley Park Drive. The bus stop we hadn't gotten off at before.

There, we could see a spectacular view of the Lions Gate Bridge.

As we looked down, about a half mile in front of us were the bridge's two lion sculptures. The view of the suspension bridge was breathtaking.

We had reached this gorgeous view of God's masterpiece by trusting him — I admit, sometimes more reluctantly than others — one step at a time.

I realized I can't always see my final destination, but if I follow God in taking the next small step, he will take me to places far better than I can ever imagine.

# WHY GOD BROUGHT ME BACK HOME

## BY SANDI BERGMAN

I grew up in a Christian home in a small town where everyone was family, and I went to a church where the pastor and my dad were best friends. Life was comfortable growing up in Iowa. But things started to change after high school.

I slowly found myself surrounded by people who lived to party, often to excess. I, on the other hand, was on a mission to be healthy and fit. I refused to eat beef after I discovered my favorite cow was missing and our freezer was full of hamburger meat and steak. I grew a huge garden (including soybeans for my meatless burgers), and I ran and rode my bike every chance I got.

I became a real outcast, especially around my siblings.

At 23, I moved to Iowa City, where I found a close group of friends who thought and acted like I did. We cooked our vegetarian meals together, bought food from the co-op, grew a garden, and rode our bikes everywhere (even though I lived 10 miles from town in a log cabin heated with wood). It was like going back to my childhood. I loved it!

We were all "good people" who followed the "rules" and treated others with dignity and respect. If you had asked any of us if we were Christian, we would have said "yes," but we didn't think or talk about it.

### RETURNING HOME

I eventually left Iowa City to move back to Des Moines to work for the family business. I was working in an office, which I hate, surrounded by the party animals I moved away from. I felt very lonely. Then I met my husband, Allen, a man of great faith and the best husband I could ever have.

We started going to church with my mom and grandma at the church Allen grew up in. It was good to be back at church, but something was still missing.

It wasn't until we found my current church that we found a true church home. There, I learned God loves me. Me! That he guides me, cares for me, watches over me. Who knew?

I started to understand that when I could provide something the church needed, it was God's plan. God came through every time there was a need, and most of the time, it was way above and beyond what I could imagine.

Many years after I moved back, while at work, I walked in on my three siblings standing around the counter in the kitchen and discussing their medication. They had diabetes and high blood pressure. As I entered the room, my brother said, "Well, obviously, this is heredity." Then he saw me.

I'm the oldest (four years older than my next brother), and I ran a half marathon at 63. I can throw hay with the best of them, and until recently, I taught fitness classes three to five times a week.

They all just walked away.

## STAYING HEALTHY

I know the path God marked out for me includes being as healthy and fit as I can be because I have 11 horses, two dogs, and six cats to care for, along with two trucking companies I help run.

As Pastor Rick Warren said, "If you're sick or dead, you can't do God's work."

Almost all of our animals are rescues, and God wants me to stay healthy so they will be cared for.

So why me? I honestly don't know the answer. I didn't really listen to God until recently. Even now, when I know God's telling me something, I argue with him once in a while over who's right, me or him.

What I do know is he always wants what's best for me, and whether I do what he asks by accident or on purpose, he still loves me. When I argue with him, he still loves me. Me!

# SURROUNDED BY GOD'S LOVE DURING HOSPICE

## BY EVELYN SHERWOOD

"We got it all," the doctors said.

"Her prognosis is good," they said.

And they were right — for a while.

Several weeks after my mom's surgery to take a tumor out of her stomach, she was admitted to the hospital, unable to hold down food, her abdomen swollen three times its average size. Her body writhed with pain.

I spent the next three weeks attempting to balance work responsibilities in Indiana and care for my mom in Michigan. I watched nurses and doctors poke, prod, and run every imaginable test on my mom with no conclusive answers. They were running out of ideas, and I was running out of patience.

Part way into week three, her oncologist approached me in the hallway, "Mrs. Sherwood, how can I help?"

"Please help me get her transferred to IU Cancer Center in Indianapolis," I said. "We need some answers."

Within the next 36 hours, Mom's paperwork was sent, a bed had opened up, and the ambulance was waiting outside to transfer her from Toledo, Ohio, to Indianapolis, a bigger city more than three hours away.

I went back to Mom's house and started throwing some of her clothes and toiletries in a suitcase, my mind swimming with questions:

"Why her? She was only 64 and had so much life left to live."

"Will cancer take her? God can heal her, but will he? She's not only my mom, but my best friend, my mentor."

"What will I do if God calls her home?"

As I drove to the IU Cancer Center in the dark of night, my mind replayed the way my folks relied on their faith during trials. I grew up watching my parents hold tight to Jesus and his promises when faced with adversity.

But now, my faith was under fire. I prayed: "Oh God, please heal Mom. I'm not ready to let her go. God, please heal my sweet momma."

## WE FINALLY GOT ANSWERS

We all arrived at the Indianapolis hospital shortly after midnight. Within two hours, this new team of doctors had discovered the answer. The oncologist walked into the room, grabbed the round black stool on wheels, and rolled it close to Mom's bed.

With tenderness, he held her hand and spoke gently. "Mrs. Steffes, we have the test results," he said. "Your body is riddled with cancer. There is nothing more we can do."

Silence hung thick in the room as time seemed to stand still. "Did she suspect this would be the prognosis?" I thought. "What was she feeling?"

I was tired, numb, and in disbelief. I could not take my eyes off of my mom, my best friend. Her body was frail, but I saw a beautiful strength rise within her. Here was my mom, at 64 years old, a pastor's wife, mother of two, grandma to six, a teacher, a Jesus lover, and everybody's biggest cheerleader. She spoke confidently.

"Doc, I know who holds my life in his hands," she said. "And I trust him completely."

The doctor and I both began to cry.

"Mrs. Steffes, I have never seen so great a faith," he said.

The next few days became a tsunami of activities. We moved my mom and dad into our small ranch home the first week of December, along with a hospital bed that resided in the northeast corner of our living room. Mom wanted to be in the living room so she could see the love pouring into our home as family and friends dropped in to give support and encouragement.

Hospice nurses and chaplains moved in and out of our home as if our front entry was a revolving door. Suddenly, I was being asked not just to be my mom's daughter, but to be her caretaker. To give her medicine every three hours through a catheter.

My thoughts raced. "What? I have no medical background." I felt as if I was on the edge of an emotional cliff. "What if I do it wrong?

I swallowed hard and exhaled a prayer, "God, please help." With that, my lesson began. Under the hospice nurse's watchful eye, hands shaking, I administered Mom's medicine for the first time.

## GOD'S LOVE DELIVERED THROUGH HIS PEOPLE

Family members and friends stepped in to help bear the weight that comes with caring for a terminally ill loved one. Food was brought, wood was chopped for the fireplace, and everyday errands were run. Still, the responsibility for administering my mom's medicine fell solely on me.

We celebrated Christmas with all the family gathered around Mom's bed. The doctors had told us it would be a miracle for her to live that long, so we were over the moon grateful that we had one final time to celebrate the birth of Jesus, her savior — our savior — together.

We laughed, cried, and savored every sacred moment.

December moved into January, and God gifted us with unexpected time. But as we watched the life fade from her daily, I could feel the toll. I had not slept more than three hours in a row, determined to get my mom her medicine to reduce her pain. I was tired. With every step I took, my body ached with exhaustion. I was beginning to question how much longer I could keep it up.

God answered a prayer he knew I needed — a prayer I never asked him for — when a friend called and asked if she could help. She had been a nurse.

"Oh, yes," I said. "Would you mind coming over to help with Mom's meds tonight?"

She arrived within an hour. A former nurse, she was ready for the task. As she pushed meds, I slept soundly for the first time in almost two months. And while I slept, someone prayed.

I am not sure who, but the next day when I woke up, I could sense the residue of prayer that hung in our home. My weary body felt renewed, restored, and regenerated. With each beat of my heart, I could feel the rhythms of grace pulsing through my veins, brought on by the prayers of God's people.

It was the grace I needed to carry me through the final week of Mom's life. We said goodbye to a woman we loved.

Mourning her loss — despite our assurances of a better life for her in heaven — still hit hard, crashing down in unexpected waves of grief.

God showed me his love in the midst of the most difficult times. And I will never forget the grace God revealed to me through his people.

# BUT GOD: WHY I NEVER SHARED MY TEEN PREGNANCY

## BY JILL DOBROWANSKY

At the age of 19, I heard three words that would change my life forever. "You are pregnant."

My boyfriend and I had only been dating for four months. At first, I was dismissive. I thought the doctor must be wrong. That it wasn't happening to me.

I thought I could ignore it and it would go away.

At the time, I had already graduated high school, was working full-time at an attorney's office answering phones, living at home with my parents, and trying to figure out what I wanted to do with my life.

We lived two houses down from where my mother grew up, in a small town in New Jersey. Everyone knew one another. You couldn't curse without your mom knowing about it by the time you arrived home.

Every Sunday, we attended the Catholic Church my family had been a part of for three generations. We typically walked to it from our first-floor apartment.

The whole town would know I was pregnant sooner or later. I was scared and embarrassed. My instinct was to run and hide.

But God. My mom knew something was wrong and put the pieces together.

It was the late 1980s, and there were options for me as an "adult."

We talked about abortion, but in my heart, I knew it was not an option I wanted to consider.

We talked about adoption, but I knew I wouldn't be able to give my baby to a well-deserving family and deal with the feelings of abandonment.

I decided the only option was to tell my boyfriend I was pregnant, keep the baby, and see what happened. Both my parents agreed that no matter what his reaction was, they were going to support me and love the baby growing inside of me.

Then the fear and shame took hold of me. Here I was, 19 years old, having to tell my 20-year-old boyfriend I was pregnant.

## ACCEPTING THE GIFT OF MOTHERHOOD

I will never forget sitting in his car and sharing the news. He was shocked and said he would need time to process it. Thoughts poured through my mind:

'What if I have to do this on my own?"

"What if he rejects me and our baby?"

"How am I going to explain this to my family and friends?"

During the next couple of days, I started to tell my family, who all had the same reaction as my parents. They were there for me and would love and support me.

I was raised in a church where I learned to fear God. Now, I ran from an all-powerful God and hid to escape his judgment. I did not pray. I did not attend Mass. I just didn't want anything to do with a God who I falsely believed looked down on pregnancy out of wedlock.

A few days passed before I heard from my boyfriend. I was terrified of what he would say. Then he called. He agreed: We were going to do this together. Although neither one of us knew what that looked like, we were going to figure it out.

In August of 1989, I gave birth to a beautiful, healthy boy. However, the seeds of shame surrounding teen pregnancy took root.

The following June, my boyfriend and I married, surrounded by family and friends. But I also began covering up my teen pregnancy, avoiding conversations, and flat-out lying about my marriage and my son.

I was not ashamed of being a mom. I loved being a young mom and wife, and I loved my son with my whole heart. But I became a master at diverting questions about the details.

## A LONG ROAD BACK TO GOD

For the next 12 years, I would continue to hide from God. I didn't pray. I didn't go to church. I just ran in the opposite direction.

But I will never forget the day the Holy Spirit spoke to my heart, telling me how everything I needed could be found if I gave God a chance.

I could feel an ever-present pull on my heart to come back to church.

I ignored this pull for months, then one Sunday, I decided to go to a church I had passed a hundred times. I finally went for services, and as I crossed the threshold of the building, I knew I was home.

Within the first 10 minutes of worship, I could feel my heart being filled, and I heard God whisper: "Welcome home, my child."

Tears ran down my face.

That September day in 2001, I opened my heart and mind and allowed God to plant the seeds of faith and salvation. There were days when I worshiped with half a heart or a distracted mind, but God began nourishing the seeds with worship, devotion, and wisdom.

However, there was still one thing he wanted me to break free from. Shame.

My teen pregnancy was something I never talked about. My husband and I didn't have any other children, so we stayed as a small family of three.

I no longer would lie about this part of my past, but I also didn't talk about it. People knew I had a son, I talked about him and his wife all the time, but I still diverted any questions about my age or his age.

But God. One evening in 2020 — in the midst of a global pandemic — I joined an online Bible study group. I knew it was time to share this part of the story I kept hidden for so long.

God gave me the words, and I could feel the presence of the Holy Spirit with me as I shared my guilt and shame with them. Thankfully, they treated my story gently and prayed with me for the strength and wisdom to share it with others.

Though we only knew each other for a few months, I felt the power of God's divine intervention. God's greater purpose for bringing this small group of women together.

Through their friendship — their love and acceptance — I felt my guilt melt away.

God's love and acceptance was always there. I was just too clouded with shame to see it.

# HOW MY FAITH IN GOD HELPED ME SURVIVE WAR AND LIFE IN A REFUGEE CAMP

## BY RICHMOND APPLETON

From an early age, I believed in the power of prayer. I grew up in a small fishing village in Liberia. It sits in Western Africa, on the bank of the Atlantic Ocean, with beautiful beaches, white sand, and lots of coconut and palm trees.

I am the youngest of seven children, and when I was five years old, I was struck by an illness that limited my body physically. But my spirit was strong.

I prayed for strength to keep up with my siblings. When I started formal education at 10 years old, I prayed to grasp the lessons I needed and not be broken by the cruel teasing of my peers.

When war forced my family to flee to a refugee camp two countries away, I prayed for a safe journey. And when it became clear the war would never allow for my family and me to return to our home, I prayed for resettlement in the United States.

### FAITH THROUGH SICKNESS

My faith has always been my foundation. I know that nothing is possible without God, and when I need him most, he is always there.

Knowing he will see me through any challenge or obstacle that comes my way truly gives me peace. And it is this peace that brought me through one of the most challenging times in my life.

When I was five years old, polio struck the left side of my body. No one knew the cause of this illness, and my family did the best they could to care for me through the paralysis.

Walking and physical activity such as running were challenging, but I was determined to do as others did — I did not want special treatment. I just wanted to be.

After a bout with polio, my mother was very protective. She worried about my safety. I remember my older sister pleading with her to allow me to start school. And she finally did, when I was 10.

It was not the experience I imagined. Students were cruel. They teased me about my advanced age and my disability, but I was determined to learn.

## THE POWER OF PRAYER AMID WAR

When civil war erupted in Liberia in 1989. My family and I were forced to flee the home where we lived for three years.

I remember the sound of gunshots in the distance as my sister and I ran through the streets of our community for safety. I remember the feeling of desperation when I lost her in the crowd. I also recall the immeasurable joy of finally finding her again.

Once we made it to the Buduburam refugee camp in Ghana, my four family members and I set our hopes on resettlement in the U.S. My older sister Alice was already in America, and we prayed to join her someday.

The refugee camp was located in the Gomoa region and is about 23 miles from Accra, the country's capital. It was crowded with families, food was scarce, and locals were not always welcoming.

Patience is one of the toughest tests of faith. When it came time to begin the process of applying for resettlement, all we could do was wait.

I knew that gaining refugee status for resettlement is one of the most prolonged processes to experience and that there would be much out of our control since it involves the United Nations and U.S. Immigration.

When the application was submitted, we were called for an interview with U.S. Immigration officials. The entire process took five years: 1999 to 2004. After our pre-screening, we were called for a follow-up. It took one year for us to find out the status of our application.

It was heartbreaking when we received the rejection letter. We explained it was unsafe to return home to no avail, so we continued to make due in the refugee camp. And we kept praying.

Though defeated by the rejection, I knew we had to keep trying. I knew God had plans for my life. My family and I applied again. And we waited, again.

Whenever doubt threatened to overwhelm me, when I felt hopeless about not being able to leave the refugee camp, I turned to Philippians 4:13: "I can do all things through Christ who strengthens me."

Through these words, God provided assurance and restored my hope and trust.

Finally, we were told we'd been approved. We were going to join my sister in the United States. It was a miracle!

My family and I arrived in Minnesota in February 2004. The freezing cold was a big culture shock for us, but we looked forward to the adventure ahead. We looked forward to a new life.

Through the trials and tests of patience, God listened to my prayers. And deep in my heart, I know he is a trusted friend.

# I SEARCHED FOR MY BIOLOGICAL GRANDMOTHER AND FOUND MY HEAVENLY FATHER

## BY POLLY GARRETT

It felt like a fairytale. After just more than two years together, Jason and I were engaged. My dreams were becoming reality and I couldn't wait for our life as a married couple to begin.

It was as though Jason was designed for me — a tall, dark, and handsome young man with a heart so generous, so kind, so accepting.

At 18, my life seemed to be filled with promise. It was July 2011, and I was about to do my A-Levels, which would qualify me for university to become a teacher. I lived in the small town of Northampton, about 70 miles northwest of London, a tiny village where everything seemed frozen in time. I was ready to broaden my horizons.

Yet one thing had been bothering me. I had grown up without my father. He did not want me to be a part of his life. Memories flashed of the times when I had tried to see him, but he ran away from that seven-year-old girl with the Christmas card.

I knew he had been adopted when he was a child, so I desperately hoped his biological family might want to be involved in my life. I even thought — if things went well and I found them — maybe they might come to my wedding.

I was longing to belong.

## QUESTIONS AND ANSWERS I WAS NOT READY FOR

I knew searching for my father's biological mother was not going to be easy, and I did not think I would find them. I thought just knowing the family name would be enough.

A paper trail was the easiest route to begin. So I bought my father's birth certificate and waited for it to arrive. Within a week, I had it in my hands — there was his birth name, and there was his mother's name. No father was written there.

I began to imagine what my grandmother was like. Was she still alive? Would she want to meet me? Did I look like her?

I searched on Ancestry.com. I tried to buy her birth certificate by guessing her date of birth, but all these routes led to a dead end. I was stuck.

Months passed, and my attention turned to wedding planning and setting a date in 2012. We decided to have our wedding in a church, although I had not set foot in one for a long while. I was not a Christian. I did not know God. We were getting married in a church because it was beautiful. It felt dreamlike.

Just as the search for my biological family was growing cold, my mother offered a suggestion: "Why don't you ask the churches in the area on the birth certificate? Churches always help."

I emailed every church in the area. One offered further help — to put an advertisement in their newsletter about my search.

Within a few weeks, I had two email responses. Both were relatives of my grandmother! I could not believe I had found her. I was beyond excited. It felt like everything was falling into place, and I was desperate to meet her.

One of the relatives emailed with pictures and a long story of my grandmother's life, of how she had been a mental health nurse and had two more children. But she was suffering from dementia in a care home. I was deflated, knowing I probably would never get to trade stories with my grandmother, but there was still hope I could know her.

## A DEVASTATING TURN OF EVENTS

On the day we set the official date for our wedding, I had a video call with the other relative, a cousin of my father's. Near the end of the call, she grew contemplative. She said, "Your grandmother has Huntington's Chorea. I can't really tell you about it, but if you look it up yourself, you will understand."

I looked it up on Google. England's National Health Service website came up. "Huntington's disease is an inherited condition that damages certain nerve cells in the brain," it said.

The word "inherited" transfixed my eyes.

My fiancé Jason was sitting next to me. My mum also came into the room. I looked at them both and said, "I could have this, it's inherited, and it says here that there is a 50/50 chance."

I decided to get in contact with my father to tell him about it. To my surprise, he decided to also be tested for the disease.

Six months later, I was holding a brown envelope with my test results. We both tested positive for Huntington's disease. If I had known Job from the Old Testament, I would have felt like him. I felt cursed.

Then my world fell apart. Jason said he needed space and wasn't sure about getting married anymore. A hellish week followed, and I begged him to speak to me. I was devastated and felt broken.

For the first time, I reached out to God for help. Slowly, I came to know him as a loving father — my perfect, loving, and always with me Heavenly Father — who was restoring me and healing me.

Jason and I began writing letters to one another to say what we could not say in person. That summer was long one, but things became clear. We loved each other despite the terrible circumstances.

After reuniting eight months later, in an intimate ceremony, Jason and I stood before the same vicar and before God. We got married in the same beautiful church. I no longer cared about wedding dresses, venues, or invites. I just wanted to marry the one who was willing to stand by me through it all.

In 2015, God restored my relationship with my father after walking through a path of forgiveness. To surprise me even more, God led my father and mother to reunite and then marry in 2017. They realized their story was unfinished.

Even though my father now has symptoms of Huntington's disease, I've had the blessing of becoming a daughter to him.

I gave my life to Jesus in 2016. I felt called to be baptized. God has walked with me through life, not death; blessings, not curses.

While my story is still unfinished, I know my Heavenly Father has more for me than even I can imagine. Despite my diagnosis, I know my future is bright.

# MULTIPLE MISCARRIAGES TURNED MY LIFE UPSIDE DOWN

## BY ANNA KETTLE

It was December 2017 when my family plans were turned upside down by a sudden and unexpected miscarriage.

As we left the hospital — after a scan confirmed my worst fears — I was devastated, and so was my husband, Andy. We had lost our baby.

We spent most of the run-up to the holiday season in a fog of sadness, going through the festive motions and feigning half smiles but unable to summon genuine joy.

It had felt like the right time to extend our family.

My son Ben was two and a half and settling into his preschool year. My husband's new business was thriving. We had just moved to a bigger family home in Liverpool, England.

I knew miscarriages were common, but I never expected it to happen to me. Once I got past my initial disappointment, I reasoned I would just take a few months to heal before trying again.

Five months later, my husband Andy and I got pregnant, and everything felt as if it was finally falling into place. I was excited about our new baby.

Then I suffered a second miscarriage. Two miscarriages within six months.

The loss hit me hard. The conversations with doctors about tests and screenings were overwhelming.

It felt so unfair. I felt angry, anxious, and undone. I spent a lot of time in tears. And I had so many questions whirling in my head.

Suddenly, nothing was certain. What if something serious was wrong? What if it happened again and again? How many times were we willing to put ourselves through this?

Our medical team advised us not to try to conceive until we had some tests at the local hospital's recurrent miscarriage clinic.

It was a small gift as it gave us some time to heal.

Then I miscarried a third time.

## STILLNESS AND SILENCE

The third miscarriage tipped us into the category of "unexplained recurrent loss."

It also came much later in my pregnancy. It was a silent miscarriage. There was no indication that something was wrong until a routine scan couldn't find a heartbeat.

Nothing. Just stillness and silence.

I couldn't believe what I was hearing, even though I was looking at the screen with my own eyes. Less than two weeks earlier, we had seen our baby with a healthy heartbeat. Everything had been fine, but now nurses ushered us into a quiet side room and offered surgery options.

We were both in shock and couldn't quite take it in. How could this be happening to us again?

I was crushed. My husband and I had prayed hard, trusted God, and felt God giving us specific promises about our child. We also believed the medical staff when they said things looked good this time.

I felt let down by God.

But perhaps what hurt most was the loss of hope for future pregnancies. We were both 39 by then. Time was no longer on our side, and our miscarriages remained "unexplained," which meant no medical answers or possible cure.

My husband and I had mixed emotions. Why was this happening to us? Where was God? Why wasn't he answering our prayers? Did he care about us at all?

I had no answers. But in the end, what else could I do except cry out to God in my brokenness?

So that's what I did. I shut my bedroom door, cried, shouted, and screamed at God. Over and over again.

And do you know what I discovered? In my darkest moments, God was there, extending his hope, peace, and comfort.

## WE PERSEVERE

It feels scary to let go of what I can't control about my life and to put my trust in God alone — rather than what I hoped my future family would look like.

Letting go of control doesn't mean I've suddenly stopped wanting a larger family. But by loosening my tight grip on this desire, I can open my hands to different possibilities and feel more relaxed about how and when that happens.

It's been a hard-earned lesson about faith. But today, I can trust my family will be the family God designs. My Father God is good, and his Word promises I can trust him.

Recurrent miscarriage is the greatest heartbreak I have ever faced, but I know God alone is my only sure hope. And it's a hope that goes beyond the grave.

# WITNESSING AND SHARING MY SON'S MIRACULOUS HEALING

## BY DAWN SCHNEIDER

It was finally time. Our favorite week of the year — family camp! We looked forward to attending Okoboji Lutheran Bible camp in Iowa every year for our family vacation, and this year was no exception.

Our son Cory has special needs, which makes it too cumbersome and difficult to stay in a hotel. Our vacation options were limited to visiting family or friends until we heard about family camp.

At camp, we made and hung out with friends, and we had awesome counselors who loved our special needs kids and their families.

This year, we were excited that camp fell on Cory's birthday, specifically the "free day" at the nearby amusement park. But the night before, Cory started vomiting.

My heart sank. Typically his vomiting doesn't stop on its own. He becomes severely constipated, needs to go to the ER, and is often admitted to the hospital. I braced myself for a long night.

After several bouts of vomiting, Cory said he wanted to sleep with me.

This is unusual because Dad is always his "go-to." Mike is so much better with medical issues. I get too caught up in what's happening to focus on Cory, but Mike zeros in on him, sings to him, plays with him, and finds creative ways to distract him.

For some reason, this time, Cory wanted me. I was delighted yet perplexed.

As we lay down, hoping to go back to sleep, I had this overwhelming urge to pray to ask God to heal Cory. And a stronger urge that God absolutely could.

## THE NUDGE TO PRAY

I placed my hand on Cory's tummy and started a conversation with God:

"Dear God. I know you can heal Cory. As you know, tomorrow is his birthday, and he is looking forward to celebrating with his camp and church friends, but I trust you. If someone at the hospital needs to meet Cory and be blessed by him, I surrender that to you."

"Just like Shadrach, Meshach, and Abednego knew you could save them from the fiery furnace, I know you can heal Cory. Even if you don't, I will trust you, worship you, and share your awesomeness with others.

"But if you do heal Cory, I will share with the entire camp what you have done."

Cory had been sick like this many times before and many more times since, but I had never felt the confidence I felt that night.

I knew God could heal Cory. In scripture, it says you must only have a mustard seed of faith to move mountains. Well, I didn't have a mustard seed of doubt God could heal Cory!

I was full of the Holy Spirit. There was no room for me, my doubt, or my thoughts. Nothing could detract from my belief and the blessing of such confidence.

As we lay there, Cory settled in, and his breathing moved into the beautiful, calming rhythm of sleep. I watched him and soaked in God's peace. I also drifted off.

When we woke up, I realized Cory's vomiting had stopped when I started praying.

God had reached down, touched Cory, and healed him. We got a great night's sleep. "Oh my goodness," I thought. "This really happened!"

It was the only time his vomiting ended without medicine or medical intervention.

## SHARING GOD'S STORY

I dreaded the next part, which was keeping my end of the bargain.

My husband and two sons love to be onstage, but not me. I love watching them, but I have never been a fan of the spotlight.

In addition, I know I can talk about God without crying, and I can talk about Cory without crying, but if I have to talk about both of them, I am a hot mess.

I approached the pastor and told him I needed a couple of minutes to share our story with the camp. And I did. It wasn't pretty, but God got the glory.

I don't know why God has blessed our family with this and other miracles, but I am so thankful he has.

Doctors said Cory was never supposed to talk, but at the age of 5 ½ he and God decided it was time. His first full sentence was, "I'm happy today."

Cory also had a heart condition, and the best the doctors said we could ever hope for was a plateau. But it got better and better until there was no evidence anything was wrong with his heart.

Some miracles were immediate, as it was at family camp. Others took years of prayers before we saw God's healing power.

Just like Jesus healed people in the Bible — God the Father, God the Son, and God the Holy Spirit still do. I am a witness to his miracles, and therefore, I want to witness.

# SEVEN DOORS IN: HOW AN UNLIKELY FRIENDSHIP BLOSSOMED IN PRISON

## BY R. A. NADERMAN

I took a deep breath and checked my documents before proceeding to the front door of the medium-security prison just two miles from my home.

Click.

The door shut behind me as I neared the second door.

Click.

I slid my papers to the guard under a security window. He looked them over and asked if it was my first time. He passed me a clipboard with a form and said: "His name, his number." I took a breath and told him.

I was here to see a man I'd never met before.

I looked around the waiting room and sat on the blue plastic sofa. I pressed my hands together to stabilize the trembling, and I thought back to a few months earlier when I had first learned about Aaron.

While sitting at lunch at work, a casual conversation with a coworker turned serious when I learned her brother was incarcerated. After hearing her story, my heart broke for her carrying such a heavy cross. The next day I gave her a card with a little bit of cash in it.

She texted me that night when she got home. She said she could not accept it. Now, when I give someone a gift, I just want them to accept it. So I told her it was for her brother, Aaron, and she agreed. A few days later, she told me Aaron wanted to send a thank you note and asked if it would be OK. I said yes.

In his note, Aaron shared a bit of his story, and I saw he had a lot of enthusiasm for Jesus. We continued to correspond, which eventually brought me to this prison to meet Aaron for the first time.

As I waited, I wondered if I would be able to maintain the conversation. I was meeting someone I didn't know. The differences between us were vast. I am a white, middle-class, working mom, and Aaron is a black man who has been in prison for 12 years.

Then I remembered a particular letter. In it, Aaron mentioned the date he was arrested — the same day I became a mother.

I remembered staring at the paper in disbelief.

It was a day I would look back on and say my life was never the same. The same was true for Aaron, but for a much different reason.

## INTO THE PRISON

My name was called, and I passed through the third door.

Click.

The guards patted me down and directed me through a metal detector.

Click.

I continued to weave my way through the prison, and I realized how alone I was. No one there knew me. My husband wasn't with me, nor were my children. No one knew my title or reputation. I had no money. I didn't even have my cell phone.

Click.

The fifth door closed behind me. When we arrived at the next door, it was a heavy iron gate. It crept slowly open to the side until there was enough room to pass through.

Click.

The sixth door was secured before the seventh door was released. I noticed a familiar, calming feeling. The feeling I had come to know as the presence of God. It occurred when I was deep in prayer or quiet in church. And now here, while walking through a prison.

Click.

When I reached the visiting room, the guard assigned me a table to wait for Aaron. I started to reflect. I thought of all the times I had driven past the prison, perhaps hundreds of times. Sometimes I saw the men exercising in the yard. Sometimes I diverted my eyes because it was too much to take in.

Sometimes I wondered: "Who was there, and what had they done?"

Other times, I thought: "What was it like on the inside? How did someone survive something like prison?"

And sometimes I grew judgmental: "Had they learned their lesson?"

Seven doors in, my observations were different. The tables around me buzzed with conversation as inmates visited family and friends. I saw their smiles and heard their laughter.

As I continued to wait, the tables around me began to make comments.

"She's been waiting so long."

"They'll hardly have time to visit. Visiting hours are almost up."

"I wonder if he even knows she's here."

I had not thought I would receive kindness and empathy from people inside the prison.

## MEETING AARON

Aaron arrived nearly 90 minutes later. He had not expected me to visit, he explained, and was surprised to meet me.

He apologized if he was a bit out of sorts, as he had just come off a three day fast. I knew he used this spiritual practice. In his letters, he said he was fasting for me and my family.

We discussed unanswered questions from our letters, and we formed a friendship as we discovered how much we had in common.

As we talked, I realized God had been and continues to be with Aaron, despite his incarceration. Just like God has been and would always be with me.

No matter what obstacle I may face, or what challenges life presented, or what poor decisions I made, God promised he would always be with me. He would not abandon me. He would not forsake me. And he never has.

# PATIENCE, PRAYER, AND IN VITRO: GOD BLESSED MY FAMILY

## BY AMY VINCELLI

Since I was young, I wanted to be a mother. So when my husband and I tried for more than a year to get pregnant without success, I started to question why.

My husband Nick and I went to a doctor in town and did as much as we could. Then we were referred to the Mayo Clinic in Rochester, Minnesota. Doctors ran tests on me. Then on my husband. The results seemed normal.

For years, I had fought my way through feelings of anger, loneliness, and unworthiness. Now, I fell into despair.

"Why wasn't I good enough to be a mother?" I thought. "Why would God not bless us with something that seemed so natural, a baby?"

At the time, I worked at a childcare center. It became so difficult to be around children when I wanted one of my own so badly. I finally left my job and took time off to stay home.

### TRUSTING GOD FOR CHILDREN

After months of procedures, my husband and I decided, along with our doctor, that our best chance to conceive would be through in vitro fertilization.

On our first try, we implanted two viable embryos. Those embryos turned into our now nine-year-old twins, Elijah and Will. They were our first little miracles.

Four years later, we held not one but two babies in our arms. A double blessing!

When the twins were 18 months old, we started trying for more children but had no luck on our own.

We knew I could have a baby. We knew it could happen. So we went back to the Mayo Clinic and decided we'd do a frozen transfer with the eggs we had already frozen after our first round of in vitro.

The first transfer didn't work, but the second one did. Then I had a miscarriage.

When we lost our baby, I thought: "Why do all of these things have to happen to me?" It was painful. I just wanted to have a family.

I didn't understand why God would give us such a perfect gift only to take it away so quickly. Infertility had broken my heart for years, and that felt horrible enough. But now we had lost a baby. The heartache seemed too much to bear. I didn't know how I would recover.

God had another plan. Three months after our miscarriage, much to our surprise, I became pregnant without medical help. It was such a great moment. We never stopped trusting God.

Nine months later, my son Caleb was born.

## GROWING OUR FAMILY WITH GOD

We had three beautiful children, but Nick and I had another choice to make. We couldn't decide if we wanted to grow our family. I decided to ask a friend how I'd know when our family felt complete.

She said: "You would just know. We're done. Clear as day."

Her words struck me. In my heart, I knew I wanted a daughter. I felt God leading me. We decided to take one more chance, this time without medical intervention.

We decided to try for three months. If it happened, it happened. If it didn't, we decided that was God's plan for our family.

Our daughter, Evelyn, was conceived within a month. She's two now. It still blows my mind how God was able to take care of me and put something this big — a family with four beautiful, healthy children — in my life.

I don't know why some women are able to have children and some are not. Why some struggle with infertility and some don't. Why medical procedures work for some and not others.

What I do know is God put something deep in my heart, and he made it happen. It might not have happened the exact way I planned, but God was with me through every step.

Today, I have a stronger understanding of God's timing and how he works everything together. In my most broken moments, God is still working, leading, and shaping me into who I am meant to be.

This makes everything sound so easy. I know it's not easy. I know the hurt and pain. But I also know he can make something good come out of anything.

# THE MIRACLE OF FEEDING THOUSANDS DURING COVID

## BY AL LAUDENCIA

I own two restaurants, a catering company, and a food trailer. When the state closed dine-in restaurants because of the COVID-19 pandemic in 2020, I freaked out. Not outwardly, of course, but I was scared.

My wife Betsy and I have three daughters, Taylor, Lily, and Emma. Our company, Big Al's BBQ & Catering, employs dozens of people. It's our livelihood. Everything is riding on our business.

Quickly, I changed our business model. We temporarily closed our 600-seat restaurant in Des Moines and decided to keep our 80-seat restaurant in Adel, a town about 20 miles west, open to drive up and take out.

We were in an impossible situation. We're close to a $3 million outfit. And we had to close just before the weekend, which is when we do 70% of our business.

I reached out to our accountant. "I don't know if we're going to make the $10,000 payroll," he said. "Your employees won't be able to get paid, and neither will you."

I didn't know what to do, so I did what I always do. I prayed.

## THE MIRACLE OF FEEDING 5,000

I pray continuously. I'm always asking God for direction.

Each morning, I get up and tell God, "Thank you." And I ask for direction, such as how he wants to use my day. And I ask God to help me let go of my expectations. To let go of what I think should be done, and to allow what God wants to be done to become clear.

I have been angry at God before, but I was past that. Was I confused? Yes. Was it uncomfortable? Yes. But I trusted. I knew God was in it with me.

As I talked to my accountant, I thought about all the meat we bought for the weekend. It was smoked up and ready to go, but our dining room was closed.

"What are you going to do, Al?" my accountant asked.

"We have two choices," I said. "We can throw it away because it's going to expire, or we could try to sell it. But that's not reasonable. We're going to give it away."

I prayed about it more, and then I put it on Facebook. We were giving away free meals.

I thought of Mark 6: 37-44. People said it was impossible. The disciples had five loaves and two fish, but Jesus fed 5,000.

I thought, "Maybe God has a reason for this."

## FEEDING EVEN MORE

That Friday night, we set up our parking lot in Adel. It looked similar to how we serve guests through our catering company, but this time each meal was free.

It was the first Friday of quarantine, we gave away free pulled pork and beef brisket sandwiches with house kettle chips. Saturday was BBQ chicken dinner with mashed potatoes and green beans.

Families lined up in our parking lot, and then people started to help, volunteering to serve meals. People started offering donations. We made payroll that week. I'm not sure how, but we did. But we weren't done.

People were offering to sponsor free meals, so we kept cooking. Local businesses started to donate what they could. Each night, we fed at least 150 people. We ran out of food and had to order more.

It started to snowball. More donations came in. News crews showed up. We cooked more meals, and more people were fed. We started offering free meals to local hospitals and police and fire departments. We fed children who qualified for free lunch at school. We fed truck drivers and other essential workers.

Here's the miracle. Our numbers were the best they've ever been. How does that happen? It didn't make sense. We were serving takeout and giving away free meals. I had fewer employees and received more.

We fed 5,000 people. But then my buddy said: "Al, what about Mark 8: 1-21?" Jesus fed 4,000 more. So we kept cooking.

It was truly a God thing. From March 20 to May 20 of 2020, we fed more than 9,700 people.

Sometimes I go to church, I listen to the pastor preach, and I read the Bible, but the stories don't always seem real. But here it was, a miracle.

I'm not sure why God blessed my business when so many others went out of business during the pandemic, but I'm so thankful he did. It was definitely the hand of God.

# APPENDIX:
# FAITH STORY RESOURCES

*"Do not fear, for I am with you; do not be dismayed, for I am your God. I will strengthen you and help you; I will uphold you with my righteous right hand." (New International Version)*

*"So don't worry, because I am with you. Don't be afraid, because I am your God. I will make you strong and will help you. I will support you with my right hand that saves you. (International Children's Bible)*

*— Isaiah 41:10*

# QUIZ: WHAT'S YOUR STORYTELLING STYLE?

G od values each of us equally. And he values our stories the same way. But many storytellers, when first being coached, don't see the value of their story.

But what if I told you that your storytelling style — your natural tendencies when processing or preparing a story — was not a judgment about the quality of your story? Would you share a true, first-person story about your faith if you knew you could overcome your storytelling weaknesses and lean into your storytelling strengths?

**The following quiz will help you identify your storytelling tendency** as either a Story Builder or a Story Carver. A Story Builder needs to build their story from the ground up, piece by piece, while a Story Carver starts with a mountain of material and has to carve chunks away to sculpt it into their story. One is not better than the other. Both tendencies are needed to share a complete story of God's work in the world and our lives.

**Story Builders start from scratch and construct their stories piece by piece.** If their story were a sculpture, they'd start with nothing and add small clay pieces until a shape forms. Story Builders often look at the mountain of material a Story Carver has and feel inadequate. That's not true; they just have a different storytelling process.

If you feel doubt as a Story Builder, you're not alone. Most Story Builders need encouragement and reassurance that their story is worth sharing. You can use the Faith Storytellers Framework as a guide and, when you follow it step by step, can better understand what to add to your story to bring it to life.

A Story Builder's weakness is also their strength. Because they start from scratch, Story Builders know how to focus their story. They naturally avoid "rabbit trails" that confuse the reader or listener, as these diversions don't connect to the story's main point.

In addition, Story Builders tend to be efficient and practical in their lives and their stories, making their stories critical to passing on hard-won wisdom on how we can connect, experience, and honor God in our everyday lives.

Many stories shared by Story Builders are like rolling hills, bringing comfort or meaning; they're easy to understand and relate to. Indeed, these are the stories that glue communities of faith together. When gathered and written, their stories can create meaningful devotions, story collections, or memoirs of faith.

**Story Carvers start with a lot of material and must whittle their story down piece by piece.** If their story were a sculpture, they'd begin with a large chunk of clay and cut out pieces until a shape emerges. Because their material carries emotional and spiritual weight, they may feel overwhelmed or distraught about their story or how it will be interpreted.

They tend to have multiple points to their story and may need help focusing on one. Refining their story's ending may be the most challenging part of the Faith Storytellers Framework, as Story Carvers often want to "hit home" their main point by elongating their ending. Instead, they should aim for a "mic drop" moment that reverberates long past the curtain closing.

Story Carvers also have strengths that initially seem like weaknesses. Story Carvers tend to share life-changing stories that resonate with their audience. Due to the events they share, tension naturally builds in their story, drawing the reader or listener in — as long as they don't release that tension before the ending.

Their story arcs tend to be sharper, with angular mountains and valleys, often depicting awe. Their journey wasn't for the faint of heart. Story Carvers not only survived their story but were strengthened and refined by it — leaving their audience grateful to hear, but not experience, their tale.

Their stories resonate and may be appropriate for a worship night or as a keynote speaker. When written as a memoir, you may find their book difficult to put down.

***Take the following quiz, or try an interactive version online at faithstoryteller.org/resources.***

## QUIZ: WHAT'S YOUR STORYTELLING STYLE?

Select the statement that best fits your natural writing or editing process. Then total how many A's and B's you chose.

**A:** I write emails by starting with the main points, adding the greeting and ending later.

**B:** I write whatever comes to mind and then go back and edit the email.

**A:** When I journal, it's typically a few sentences, if that.

**B:** I have notebook after notebook of journals.

**A:** It seems as though I don't have a story to tell.

**B:** It seems as though I'm drowning in the material and don't know where to start.

**A:** When I send a text message, it's typically brief and to the point.

**B:** I've been accused of sending a novel when I text.

**A:** When I crack a joke, it's brief and to the point.

**B:** My humorous tales take long and winding roads.

**Total A:** _____

**Total B:** _____

### *Mostly A's:* Story Builder

You may feel as if you don't have a story to tell, but that's not true. You tend to start from scratch and will need to add to the story to build it into a fuller narrative. At a minimum, aim for 700 words or, if spoken, six minutes long.

- **Stay focused on your story** and how God is at work. Don't worry about the stories of others or how much material they have to work from.

- **Talk it out.** Many Story Builders are verbal processors who clarify their thoughts through conversation before they know what they think. If you've ever said, "I need to talk this out," you'll benefit from asking a friend to talk through your story to explore and understand it. Find someone who can listen intently and ask meaningful, open-ended questions to probe what happened in your story, how you responded, and how you felt at the time. As you "talk it through," you may share details you find interesting, but don't align with your Story Anchor, or main point of your story.

- **Find a listener.** Look for someone you trust who will receive what you share generously and with an open heart. They'll give you the benefit of the doubt, empathize with your struggles, and affirm your emotional response before asking challenging questions about your story. You're looking for someone who is working on themselves and is growing in their own right, regardless of their age or occupation. Someone willing to interrupt a rambling anecdote by asking, "What does that mean to you?" or "How did you feel in the moment?" or "How does that connect to your story?"

- **Start with an outline.** You'll see where you need to add to your story.

- **Building your story may feel like heavy lifting.** It's hard work creating a story from scratch. Find a way to enjoy watching your story unfold before your eyes.

- **Add details to your story that are relevant to your Story Anchor.** Share more than you might otherwise if left to your own devices.

- **Consider sharing your story with a trusted friend or loved one.** Ask what questions they have or if they need clarification on any parts of your story. It's often easier for someone else to see what pieces should be added.

### *Mostly B's:* Story Carver

You may feel overwhelmed by your material or your story's magnitude, and you may not know where to start. Remember, you have agency over your story. You are the story's keeper, meaning you can carve it down to its essence. At most, write 1,200 words or speak it in less than eight minutes.

- **Stay focused on the one story you feel called to share.** You may have multiple stories in your material, so select and stick to one story that makes one point about God.

- **Write it out first.** Many Story Carvers are internal processors who benefit from alone time and personal reflection. "I need to think about it" is a common response, especially if you're prone to "coming up blank" when asked a question you haven't mulled over. Reflecting on and writing your story can help you find agency as you write it out, allowing you to control how much or how little to share. Ask yourself how you responded to the events in your story, how you felt as you processed it over time, and how you took action — however small — to grow.

- **Write with a different point of view.** Look for ways to distance yourself from your story, which will shift your perspective and allow you to see your story from a different point of view. Try writing in the third person. Narrate your story with kindness and compassion and a heart so large that no amount of pain or suffering could overwhelm the writer. Imagine a gentle yet strong embrace. A narrator who wants to feel your feelings with you. Who will sit with you as you reflect. Who will challenge you to discover one and only one Story Anchor. They'll guide you to a piece of glimmering silver that was raked through the fire, a silver that was shaped by the heat yet never burned

- **Accept that you will not use most of your material** as you will whittle away everything that is not directly supporting or leading to your Story Anchor. You may leave so much out that you decide to write a different story at a later time.

- **Resist the urge to keep pieces of your story that don't align with your Story Anchor.** Honor all of your story, and then carefully select which details or phrases to use. Try phrases on as if trying on clothes in a store. A phrase may look great on the page, but when spoken out loud — a writer's or speaker's way of trying something on for size — you'll want to select the most comfortable fit.

- **Share your story with a trusted friend or loved one.** Ask where they get confused and what isn't relevant to this particular story. Their feedback will help you edit your story down to an appropriate length.

## WORKING WITH YOUR STORYTELLING STYLE

As you reflect on your storytelling style, consider ways your tendency might work for you. For example:

- **You love writing and keep a journal.** Consider flipping back through the pages to refresh your memory.

- **You're not a fan of writing and are more comfortable speaking.** Find a friend or loved one who can listen. Consider having them take notes or record and transcribe your story, which you can edit into your first draft.

- **You can recall dates and details** such as what someone was wearing or what they said. Write these details down to see if they have a place in the story.

- **You need help remembering.** Seek out ways to activate your memory, such as looking at old photos, having a conversation that reminisces about a particular time, or recalling an event such as Christmas or a birthday, which may be clearer in your mind and can help trigger your memory.

- **You process quickly.** Keep a separate document with notes. By keeping memories or anecdotes in a different place, you can be selective about which ones fit your Story Anchor.

- **You think clearly when given time to reflect.** Get at least one good night's sleep between each story draft, if not more. Fresh eyes and seeing the story in a different format, such as on paper instead of a computer screen, can help.

244 | Mackenzie Ryan Walters

# FAITH STORYTELLERS FRAMEWORK

**E**veryone has a faith story, and the Faith Storytellers Framework can help you tell it well. More importantly, it can help your listener or reader understand and follow your story.

**The framework helps you incorporate universal storytelling elements,** such as a beginning, middle, and ending. It helps ensure your audience tracks the chronology and jumps in time or place. And it ensures you're sharing key details that help your story and God's handiwork come to life.

Find additional resources on writing, storytelling, and faith at **faithstoryteller.org/resources**.

### FAITH STORYTELLERS FRAMEWORK

**Step 1:** Pray for guidance on what true, first-person story to share about your faith.

Consider praying, "God, what story have you given me to share with others as a gift, with no expectation of return?"

**Step 2:** Outline your story into three scenes: a beginning, a middle where something changes, and an ending that shares your beliefs about God. Often, your beginning will be the opposite of your resolution.

The last part of your story is your Story Anchor or central point. Limit yourself to one. Your ending should stay in the first person through the last word. If you're unsure, try finishing with the phrase: "What I know to be true about God is …"

**Step 3:** Create a narrative sequence in each scene using this format: description (time and place), action, and reaction.

Add details using one of your five senses (touch, hearing, smell, taste, sight).

**Step 4:** Add divine details that show how God revealed himself to you.

Refine your story and check it against the Faith Story Guardrails. Review your spelling, grammar, and word usage.

**Step 5:** Prepare your story to share. Practice saying it out loud from memory if you plan to speak it. Read it out loud to yourself if you are sharing it through writing.

Ask a trusted friend what parts can be refined for clarity. Depending on your storytelling style, which is discussed in the Appendix, you may need to add to or cut parts from your story.

*Find additional resources on writing, storytelling, and faith at faithstoryteller.org/resources.*

# FAITH STORY GUARDRAILS

The Faith Story Guardrails will confirm if you've applied the concepts of the Faith Storytellers Framework, and we encourage you to review this list before you share your story.

**These guardrails will keep the storyteller, the people in their story, and those receiving their story safe.** Even storytellers with the best intentions can unintentionally hurt someone through their story. Faith stories should honor you, the people around you, and God.

**In today's polarizing environment, the Faith Story Guardrails will help you share your story** with individuals who are less receptive to faith, people who may have built spiritual fences.

While guardrails keep people safe, fences keep people out. Like physical fences, spiritual fences often address a specific challenge: Perhaps a person experienced "church hurt" or became wary of all Christians after a challenging or judgmental experience with a few. They may have grown up without a religious background or currently practice a different faith.

Keeping your story in first person — especially at the end of your story, when it's tempting to incorporate "you" or "we" — is countering your audience's apprehension with personal conviction. While arguing about theology is easy, arguing with a personal story is difficult.

**First-person stories are a bridge that can connect two opposing sides,** especially if you are intentional about what to include and what to leave unsaid. That's why these guardrails are so helpful. By checking your story against them, you can structure it to be received by any audience, regardless of where they are in their spiritual journey.

## FAITH STORY GUARDRAILS

- **I feel peace about how my story has unfolded so far.** I can share my story with composure and compassion.

- **I am willing to share my story with courage and vulnerability.** I am an imperfect person in a relationship with imperfect people. I have a perfect God.

- **I can share my story in a "PG" or "PG-13" way.** It may include the darkness, but it doesn't dwell on it. Instead, it focuses on how God worked in the situation or the light he brought.

- **My story is safe for me and the people in my story.** It does not allege wrongdoing by another or criticize or condemn others. It aligns with my church values and beliefs.

- **If needed, I am comfortable using a metaphor** instead of dwelling on the dark details or how I was wronged. Instead, I may focus on how I felt and name the emotions I was experiencing at the time.

- **I am the keeper of my story.** Because of this, my story is in the first person throughout. It uses "me," "my," "mine," and "I."

- **My story avoids teaching** or telling others what to do or what to believe ("you" or "your"). I've framed these, instead, as my approach to living or my personal belief or conviction.

- **My story avoids preaching,** which explains common beliefs or spiritual truths that universally apply ("our" or "we"). I've framed these, instead, as my personal belief about how God works in the world.

- **My story focuses on my relationship with God, not other people.** My Story Anchor, or main point, is grounded in my relationship with God and how he revealed himself to me.

- **I have only one main point in my story,** which is in my resolution. I acknowledge I have many stories to share, but I am focusing on only one.

- **My story brings resolution to the beginning.** My story's ending may be the opposite of my story's beginning. It concludes in the first person and answers the question: What do I know to be true about God that I didn't before?

- **I have agency over how long or short it is.** I have decided to share a short story that is 700 to 1,200 words when written or six to eight minutes when spoken.

- **I am ready to give my story away as a gift.** My story's value is not based on the number of people who read or hear it, nor is its value based on how people react after I share it. God already values my story.

*Find additional resources on writing, storytelling, and faith at faithstoryteller.org/resources.*

# NOTE TO READERS

It's my hope that this book inspires you to craft and share a faith story: with friends or family, with your church or community, with the wider world.

**If you enjoyed this book, please go on Amazon and leave an honest review.** I would love to hear how the stories in this book affected you or how you might apply the Faith Storytellers Framework. You can also go to **faithstoryteller.org/review**.

LEAVE A REVIEW

As an avid reader and now as an author, I know how vital reader reviews are in deciding what book to read next. Reader reviews give books credibility, and I didn't realize how much until I started this publishing journey. Taking a minute or two to share a thought or insight about this book is more helpful than you may realize.

You can play a crucial role by helping share this book with others, such as suggesting it for your book club, reading it as part of a small group, or recommending it to a friend.

I don't see "Faith Storytellers" as a book so much as an invitation. I hope you do, too. Give a friend your copy. Pass it along. Write an encouraging note on the cover page or tuck a "thinking of you" card inside: "You have an amazing story to share when you're ready."

To help encourage your faith storytelling journey, I've put additional resources online at **faithstoryteller.org/resources**.

**In addition, many Faith Storytellers have websites and books that expand on their stories.** You can find more information about each writer in the biographies section. Please reach out directly to these authors to learn more. And if you read one of their books, please leave them an honest book review as well!

- Mackenzie Ryan Walters

# SUBMIT YOUR FAITH STORY

Are you inspired to write a true, first-person story of faith?

Submit your story to be considered for upcoming Faith Storytellers books, which will feature collections of short stories around specific topics or themes.

Learn more at **faithstoryteller.org/resources**.

Submit Your Faith Story

# BIOS OF FAITH STORYTELLERS

**Richmond Appleton** works as a data analyst in the health care industry and is the author of the book "Finding Peace: A Refugee's Story From Peril to Protection." He lives in California with his wife and their three children.

**Sandi Bergman** works for her family trucking company along with her husband, daughter, and son-in-law. She lives on her dream farm near Dallas Center, Iowa, with her husband, three dogs, six cats, and 10 horses. A fitness instructor for many years, Sandi keeps fit by working on the farm and taking the dogs for walks.

**TaLeiza Calloway-Appleton** is a media professional with experience in journalism and marketing. An Ohio native, she has written for major daily newspapers, weekly news outlets, magazines, and nonprofit organizations. She lives in the Bay Area of California with her husband, Richmond, and her three children.

**Amanda Chirelli** lives in Tuckerton, New Jersey, with her parents, grandmother, and aunt. She's worked as a branch greeter at Investors Bank for 12 years and is passionate about advocacy and public speaking.

**Meghan DeWalt** is a wife, mother, and author redeemed to help others remember God. You'll find her working as a remote administrative assistant in the margins, practicing hospitality, and thoroughly enjoying seminary life as her husband works on his master's with the aim of pastoral ministry. She's written four Christian romance books, including her popular novella, "Wrapped in Red."

**Jill Dobrowansky** resides in Manahawkin, New Jersey, with her husband of 30 years, Eric. Together, they have one son who recently married the woman of his dreams. Jill has been a teacher and administrator in the public school system for 18 years. She is part of her church's leadership team for Wonderfully Made Ministry and Night to Shine Prom. She loves to read, cook, and spend time outdoors. Find her online at **plantpoweredpantry.wordpress.com**.

**Heather L. Eberhart** is a speaker and author of "Military Wife Field Manual: Finding Your Place in His World." She wears many hats as a triplet mom, mom of four, and Navy wife of more than 10 years. When she's not in stay-at-home-mom mode, she enjoys leading worship at her local church, sewing, and eating pizza on Fridays. Though the Navy uproots her often, Heather and her family currently live in Chesapeake, Virginia. Find her at **heatherleberhart.com**.

**MaryBeth Eiler** is a writer who encourages people to hold on to hope as they encounter unexpected challenges in life. As a rare disease warrior, MaryBeth found God's provision in her weakest moments and the grace she needs to endure. MaryBeth shares encouragement at **marybetheiler.com**.

**Amy Eilers** is passionate about improving population health and recently retired from a 33-year career in healthcare at Merck & Co., Inc. She and her husband hiked the 500-mile El Camino de Santiago across northern Spain in the fall of 2022 and are always looking for the next great adventure in travel. She lives in West Des Moines, Iowa, with her husband Mike, a cat, and a dog, and loves spending time with their two adult sons.

**Kerrah E. Fabacher** is a writer, coach's wife, mom, champion of three little diva girls (and three in heaven), bookworm, and "Gilmore Girls" ride-or-die. She is a Southern girl who could sit on a back porch looking over the water all day (in her dream world). Her days are spent as a licensed professional counselor right outside of New Orleans, Louisiana. Her passion is to see women take off their masks and live authentically before God, self, and others so they can experience connection and know the truth can set them free. Find her at **kerrahfabacher.com**.

**Jana Fraley** is a Wyoming ranch wife, mom, and Christian writer. She loves all things Western: art, music, books, skies, and people. When not writing, you will find her working cattle in the corral with her family, cleaning a barn or chicken coop, or having deep faith conversations over coffee with her adult daughter. Plus, she loves helping her son with his 4-H projects, cheering him on in the rodeo arena, or riding her horse in the hills and valleys of their McCormick Creek Ranch. Find her at **rusticandredeemed.com**.

**Polly Garrett** is a writer, wife to Jason for nearly eight years, and dog momma to Chihuahua Beatrix. She lives in Northampton, England, and when she is not writing, she is reading, in particular Christian fiction. She shares about her journey with writing and God at **pollythekingdomcreative.com.**

**Russell E. Gehrlein** is a retired master sergeant in the U.S. Army and a husband, father, grandfather, blogger, and author of "Immanuel Labor — God's Presence in our Profession: A Biblical, Theological, and Practical Approach to the Doctrine of Work." He is an ordinary man who is passionate about helping others experience God's presence and integrate their Christian faith at work. You can read more of his work online at **regehrlein.wordpress.com**.

**Juliana Gordon** is a pastor's wife and lives in Southern California. You can find her at **hopefilledfaith.com**.

**Beth Haag** was blessed to be a caretaker during her dad's 25-year battle with an undiagnosed neurological disorder. A fourth-generation Des Moines, Iowa, native, Haag teaches strategic written and visual communication classes at her alma mater, Iowa State's Greenlee School of Journalism and Communication. Beth can be found watching the Hallmark Channel or her favorite sports team, the Chicago (and Iowa) Cubs, along with her fox terrier, Lilly, who sings whenever she hears "Go Cubs Go."

**Diane Haskins** works at Mercy College of Health Sciences in Des Moines, Iowa, providing programming and resources for students. She is also the co-owner of Inspired Things Studio, a small business where she designs and sews one-of-a-kind clothing for women and children. She loves traveling out of state to visit her children and grandchildren and is looking forward to the day when she can move closer to them. Diane resides in West Des Moines, Iowa, with her husband, Ralph, her dog, Sir Basil the Brave (aka Sweet Basil), and her cat, Dot.

**Carrie M. Holt** is a writer, speaker, and podcaster. She is passionate about encouraging mothers of special needs children to identify, accept, and thrive in the grieving cycle that is part of the special needs journey. She co-hosts a podcast, speaks to various groups, and volunteers at her local children's hospital. She wrote a chapter in the book "Your Next 30 Days of Relationships," on what to do when your child suffers. She can be found at **carriemholt.com**.

**Pat Jacobs** passed away on Nov. 21, 2023. She wanted her celebration of life to be a party — she asked friends and family to wear tie-dye. But more importantly, she wanted to point people to Jesus. Pat was a dearly loved wife, mother, grandmother, and friend. A former mortgage loan officer and Lutheran youth director, she enjoyed being in various book and Bible studies. In retirement, she enjoyed living in West Des Moines, Iowa, with her husband, Mark and spending time camping and hanging out with family, especially their grandchildren.

**Mary Grace Johnson** lives in Tea, South Dakota, where she resides with her husband. She is semi-retired but still substitute teaches at Sioux Falls Christian School, writes at home, and sells Usborne Books & More products. Mary Grace graduated from the University of Sioux Falls with a bachelor's degree in English and a master's degree in reading. She also has a library media specialist endorsement. She has two married children and three grandchildren who are the loves of her life.

**Abbie Kampman** is living her dream as a high school English teacher, illuminating the power of the written word to her students. She and her husband of 17 years live in Grimes, Iowa, with their five sons. In her free time, Abbie loves reading, running, baking, and attending all her children's (many!) sporting events.

**Mary Potter Kenyon** discovered God had further plans for her life when he asked her to pray for her "future husband" in the summer of 2018. Three years later, Mary met that man, Nick Portzen. They're now married and live in Dubuque, Iowa. Mary graduated from the University of Northern Iowa and is a certified grief counselor. She is the author of seven books, including "Refined by Fire: A Journey of Grief and Grace," and "Called to Be Creative: A Guide to Reigniting Your Creativity." She hosts workshops and speaks on the topics of creativity, grief, and writing. Learn more at **marypotterkenyon.com**.

**Anna Kettle** is a Christian writer, blogger, speaker, and award-winning marketing professional who lives in the beautiful waterfront city of Liverpool, England, with her husband, Andy, and son Ben. Anna is a recurrent miscarriage warrior, a coffee lover and bookworm, a travel enthusiast, a gatherer of people, and a big believer in the healing power of words. Her book is "Sand Between Your Toes: Inspirations for a Slower, Simpler, More Soulful Life." Find her at **annakettle.com**.

**Al Laudencia** owns Big Al's BBQ & Catering. He lives with his wife and three daughters in Adel, Iowa.

**Sonya Joy Mack** has treated grief and illness for more than 15 years as a physician assistant. Her book, "This Changes Everything: When Death No Longer Has the Final Say," is a story of hope, humor, and healing for those who grieve, as well as encouragement to follow God-given dreams. Sonya lives in Des Moines, Iowa, with her husband and two spunky daughters, where she enjoys red wine, dark chocolate, big hugs, and living room dance parties. Connect with her at **sonyajoymack.com**.

**Vanessa May** is a semi-retired rehabilitation counselor who enjoys knitting, crocheting, road trips, and attending her grandkids' activities. She lives in Des Moines, Iowa, with her husband, John, and her tiny Morkie named Minnie.

**Lynne Modranski** is an author, speaker, and biblical life coach with a passion for inspiring and empowering others. A pastor's wife, she leads worship and small groups at a small church in northern West Virginia. When she's not writing, you'll find her enjoying her husband, daughters, and granddaughters. You might even catch her in a kayak or on a golf course. Find her at **lynnemodranski.com**.

**R. A. (Becky) Naderman** is a speaker and author. She wrote "Walk With Me," which explores race, friendship, and faith. Becky studied at St. Ambrose University, graduating with a degree in occupational therapy and psychology. Her career as an occupational therapist has allowed her to encounter people from all walks of life. She lives in Des Moines, Iowa, with her husband and three children. Connect with her at **ranadermanwalkwithme.com**.

**Jen Nelson** lives and works in West Des Moines, Iowa, with her husband, Scott, and boys Andrew and Michael. Her family and friends have formed Team Michael to raise money for the Epilepsy Foundation.

**Nicole Pilgrim** is a wife, mother, and full-time writer living in northern Colorado. She enjoys writing about life through the lens of hope, grace, and humor. She loves hiking and skiing with her family, movie nights at home that include takeout and pajamas, and a great cup of coffee first thing in the morning. Connect with her at **nicolepilgrim.com**.

**Kari Schulte** grew up in West Des Moines, Iowa, where she still lives with her husband, Rich. She enjoys volunteering, traveling, and spending time with friends and family. She has two adult children, Sam and Kelli, and a spoiled dog, Suzi.

**Dawn Schneider** works as an executive assistant and enjoys leading Bible study, praying, and spending time with family and friends. She lives in Waukee, Iowa, with her husband, Mike, and they have two grown sons. As a mother of a son with special needs, she's passionate about sharing with other parents the blessings and joy of having a child with special needs.

**Evelyn Sherwood** is a trusted soul-care guide, speaker, and blogger in Kokomo, Indiana, who has served in pastoral ministry for 35 years. Sherwood's Stories of Hope events draw a diverse audience of hundreds from the Midwest. On a summer evening, you might spot Evelyn and her husband, Steve, driving through Indiana farmlands in a canary yellow '47 Ford pickup or enjoying an outdoor movie night with their eight grandkids. Connect with her at **evelynsherwood.com**.

**Tracy Souza** is a child of grace, a mama to a not-so-little miss and mister, a retired high school teacher, a collector of many things, and a pattern and fabric designer. In 2019, her life took an unexpected turn when her marriage of almost 24 years ended. As that season of grief began to unfold, she found herself merging more of her faith into her design work and pursuing her love of writing with the goal of building community, one story and one stitch at a time.

**David Strege** is a senior financial planner at Syverson Strege in West Des Moines, Iowa. David and his wife, Jennifer, have two adult children, Erik and Adrienne, and have fostered 27 children over the years. In addition to volunteering at Wildwood Hills Ranch, David plays competitive volleyball on the national and international level. Learn about Syverson Strege at **onlyworkforyou.com**.

**Jon Thompson** is an owner and operator with a major transportation carrier and co-owner of Scoots Transportation. He has been in recovery since 2017 and believes God has given him the resilience to keep going, even when times are tough. He lives in Iowa and enjoys old cars, telling dad jokes, architecture, and learning how things work.

**Keela Dee Vaughn** is a Christ-follower, wife, writer, Texan, minimalist, and lover of all things nerdy or brewed. Her hope is to love God and others through her "subcreations," which is a term she got from Tolkien, meaning the creations she makes as a subset within God's primary world. Find her at **kdsubcreations.wordpress.com**.

**Amy Vincelli** is a busy mom of four children who works part time from home in Owatonna, Minnesota. She owns Vincelli Designs & Decor, where she handletters painted, personalized wood plaques and custom orders. Amy loves spending time with family and friends, traveling, exploring, photography, decorating, arts and crafts, and music. Connect with her at **amycoxvincelli.blogspot.com**.

**Andy Walters** is a carpenter and foreman who also serves as a master sergeant in the Iowa Air National Guard. He enjoys biking, playing bass in the worship band, and spending time with his family watching movies and camping. He lives in West Des Moines, Iowa, with his wife, Mackenzie, who edited this book, two sons, and dog Maddie.

**Tim Walters** is a lifelong journalist who serves as a state sports editor for the USA Today Florida Sports Network, overseeing the sports sections of Florida Today and the Florida Times-Union. Tim also has an extensive background in covering space. He's sat in two space shuttle orbiters, was involved in coverage of NASA's Curiosity Mars rover landing, and has created an award-winning documentary on Apollo 11 that can be found on Amazon Prime. Tim and his wife of 15 years have an 8-year-old daughter and live in Melbourne, Florida. Tim loves to run and enjoys taking part in a bowling league.

**Courtney Grace Watson** encourages women to embrace their need for community and dependence on God in all aspects of life. Courtney is an accountant for the Nashville Predators and co-leader of the Nashville community group of 4word Women. When she's not crunching numbers or writing words, she spends her time watching hockey, eating ice cream, or dreaming of a white Christmas. Connect with her at **courtneygracewrites.com**.

**Elyse Webb** is an educator at a local public school district. She is currently pursuing her Ph.D. in educational leadership. Her hobbies outside of education include cycling, throwing clay, traveling, and trying new restaurants in and around Des Moines, Iowa.

# INDEX OF FAITH STORIES

# ACKNOWLEDGMENTS

I'm grateful to Andy Walters for being my husband, my encourager, and my rock. This book took root while we were dating, and you have seen me through the ups and downs of the writer's journey.

I had fallen in love with live storytelling while working as a journalist but had stepped down from leading the newspaper's live storytelling series. You encouraged me to bring this idea to our church and then supported me as I transitioned to sharing stories online through **faithstoryteller.org**. When the nudge to put this book together came during an Alpha class, you believed it was the right thing to do. Thank you.

I'm grateful to my family, especially my stepsons, Brayden and Myles, who have brought so much joy and love into my life. I'm also grateful to our family, including my parents and siblings, as well as Andy's parents and siblings.

I'd like to thank Megan, an Arizona journalist who hatched the idea for the Storytellers Project and brought it to the Des Moines Register. You shaped my perspective of storytelling and helped me put my understanding of story structure to such good use.

Thank you to the journalism professors, editors, and colleagues who shaped my writing and my journalism career. I'm especially thankful to Amy, Wendell, Rene, John, Dan, Bob, Mara, and Carol. It was a privilege to work with you.

This book has been the product of so many encouraging words and prayers. Thank you to my friends Michelle and Dawn, who spent hours talking and praying with me. Our time together is so precious.

Thank you to the volunteer editors of this book, including Andy, Dawn, Pat, and Jessy. Having someone to share this book in draft form has meant so much.

This book wouldn't be what it is today without the beta readers, advanced readers, last-minute editors, and others who reassured me as we neared publication. Thank you.

Thank you to the team who helped make this book a reality and who helped bring it into the world. K, you are the best designer I've worked with. I can see the audience in your branding and design. Anna, you see the story that lies underneath. You're a talented writer and coach. Dee and Escher, thank you for being "finishers" on parts of this project. Kurt and Stephanie, thank you for your keen eye and attention to detail. I can't tell you how much I appreciate your copyediting skills and unwavering commitment to quality. Olivia, thank you for guiding the launch and promotion of this book in your in between.

Thank you to the pastors at my church, Lutheran Church of Hope, especially Jeremy, Pat, Richard, and Andy, and thank you also to Amanda, who led the creative arts ministry and spent so much time and energy helping me refine and present the faith storytelling class. Your guidance and grounding in faith made this possible. Thank you, also, to the prayer ministers at our church who taught me about prayer.

I especially want to thank the students in the faith storytelling classes I lead at our church. You trusted me to guide you through a faith storytelling process, and I know how vulnerable that can be. It's been amazing to hear how you continue to share your story.

Thank you, also, to the 40 Faith Storytellers who contributed a story to this book. Your example of how to tell a true, first-person story in a short format is inspiring. I know God is blessing so many through the gift of your story. You may never know the impact your story has until you get to heaven. Please know, your story already has resonated and will continue to resonate. Thank you.

# ABOUT THE AUTHOR

Mackenzie Ryan Walters is a national award-winning journalist, ghostwriter, and owner of StoryStruck Marketing. She offers book outlining workshops for aspiring memoir and nonfiction authors as well as full-service ghostwriting for aspiring nonfiction authors who lack the time or skill to craft their stories.

Mackenzie's journalism career spanned multiple states and mediums. She covered a presidential candidate's campaign for one of the top newspapers in the country, reported a 30-minute television documentary that took her inside NASA and recorded radio stories for an NPR affiliate. She co-founded and launched a live storytelling series, wrote for a national education magazine, and won recognition as a state and local newspaper reporter.

Originally from Minnesota, Mackenzie attended American University in Washington, D.C., earning a bachelor's degree in print journalism and economics. She now lives in West Des Moines, Iowa, with her husband, their two boys, and their dog, Maddie. She enjoys volunteering as a youth group leader, gardening, and baking bread.

Connect with Mackenzie at mackenzie@storystruckmarketing.com.